lead AS YOU LIVE, *live* AS YOU LEAD

*Discovering the Six Principles
of Uncommon Sense
for Uncommon Success*

AuthorHouse™
1663 Liberty Drive, Suite 200
Bloomington, IN 47403
www.authorhouse.com
Phone: 1-800-839-8640

AuthorHouse™ UK Ltd.
500 Avebury Boulevard
Central Milton Keynes, MK9 2BE
www.authorhouse.co.uk
Phone: 08001974150

First published by AuthorHouse 3/19/2007

ISBN: 978-1-4259-9175-3 (dj)
ISBN: 978-1-4259-9174-6 (sc)

Library of Congress Control Number: 2007901366

Printed in the United States of America
Bloomington, Indiana

This book is printed on acid-free paper.

lead AS YOU LIVE, *live* AS YOU LEAD

Discovering the Six Principles
of Uncommon Sense
for Uncommon Success

by Dr. Greg Sipes

with Ken Honeywell

nextv**oi**ce
CONVERSATIONS FOR LEADING

In memory of my friend and business partner
Steve Bojrab, M.D.

You led me in your living and in your dying.
I will never see leading in the same way again.

We wish to thank our wives, Markine and Becky, for patiently
supporting us throughout this project. Thanks also to our friends
Chris Wirthwein, who encouraged us and served as our editor, and
Mark Duffin, who challenged us by saying we'd never get it done.
If it weren't for the two of you, we'd have never met. And thanks to
so many others who read and re-read the manuscript until it was
shaped into its present form. A special thanks to Richard Harrison
Bailey/The Agency and to Rick and Tammy Bailey, specifically,
for their generosity in offering us the opportunity to work with
Tom Walker and Sam Waterson to design the presentation of this book.
What a wonderful experience it has been.

FOREWORD

In his intriguing new book, *A Whole New Mind: Moving from the Information Age to the Conceptual Age*, Daniel H. Pink says the new era we are entering will be characterized by "right brain" processes as opposed to the "left brain" functioning of the more technical information age that we are exiting. These days left brain functioning is being done more efficiently and effectively by computers. "Right-directed thinking", as Pink calls it, is uniquely human and is about design and interpersonal relationship. My marketing friends have pointed out that what this means for business is that relationship is taking center stage. Design is really about our relationships to concepts and so businesses that flourish in this new era will be all about relationships to concepts and to other people.

We've long known that healthy personal lives are about the right brain functioning, although we don't usually think of it this way. Right-directed thinking is inclined toward empathy, play and meaning, in other words, relationships. In our personal lives nothing is more important than our relationships with family and friends.

So for the first time in American life we are encouraged to be relational at work as well as at home because it's what works best in both settings. No longer does the employee have to put on a different hat at work from the one they wear at home. No longer can we explain non-relational work decisions as "just business" because non-relational decisions at work are just as misguided and self-defeating as non-relational decisions at home. No longer is success at work about being primarily numbers focused and making "hard nosed" decisions while success at home is about being "soft hearted." No longer can we afford to live in duplicity. We must *lead as we live and live as we lead.*

And this change requires not a new way of thinking, for that is left-brain oriented, but a new way of "seeing", a change of heart and soul. This is a change in "how" we see. With new sight, new vision, new perspective, eyes of the heart. And, of course, how we see determines "what" we see. Seeing with left brain perspective is about analyzing and managing, it's about numbers and circumstances but seeing with the right brain is about relationship, it's about engaging and influencing those around us whether at home or at work. And finally, how we see determines what we see and what we see determines what we "will" do. Our actions change because we see our world differently.

Years ago I read that when you leave home for work you should never leave your heart behind. The advice given at that time was that if your job required you to do so then you ought to consider changing jobs. Today this advice is more than a matter of your work settings preference. It actually has to do with becoming and remaining a cutting edge professional in this new Conceptual Age. This change will determine who flounders and who flourishes at work, at home and in life.

TABLE OF CONTENTS

INTRODUCTION

How Can We Possibly Need *Another* Book on Leadership?

For the past four decades, I've been reading books on leadership; I've had to. In my career as a psychologist and senior partner at one of the largest mental health practices in the Midwest, I've counseled everyone from the most down-and-out teenagers to the wealthiest, most successful corporate executives—and people from all walks of life in between. In all cases, the idea of "leadership" has seemed especially important to me. Many of these people are considered to be leaders. Others are, in some way, looking to be led out of the situations that have brought them to me in the first place.

So, I've studied the material. And, as you probably know, there are *thousands* of books on leadership. Hundreds published since the turn of the century. Dozens written each year. New ones appearing on best-selling lists every quarter. It seems that many of us are hungry for knowledge about what makes good leaders tick and how we can become better leaders ourselves.

Many of these books are excellent. Among them are the profiles of prominent business leaders and analogy books that offer leadership lessons based on the lives and teachings of great historical figures (and pop-culture icons). And there are books by football and basketball coaches, and popular books that offer prescriptive formulae for honing leadership skills and the academic studies meant to provide some empirical evidence or objective guidelines for what makes a leader great. From all of these tomes, you can get a lot of good advice.

So, why are you reading this?

Why is everyone still looking for the next leadership book? Why has no one come up with the magic bullet that will make you a great leader? Perhaps more intriguing, why in the face of *all this material* do we continue to have a shortage of real leaders these days?

I have some ideas about that. In fact, not long ago, I was convinced I had some ideas that I'd never really seen addressed in all the leadership books I've read, over the decades that I've been reading them. These ideas were based on the work I've done with people from all walks of life over the past 25 years—more than 60,000 hours of listening to patients and trying to help them understand and deal with the challenges in their lives. (That's about seven years' worth of listening, 24 hours a day, without a break for dinner or a nap.) I thought my ideas were totally unique, at least in the leadership arena. My ideas veer away from the practical and toward the, well, mystical.

They've got far more to do with *what you are* than *what you do*. My concern was that they are so unique that they'd seem outlandish. A little airy-fairy, even.

Then, something interesting happened. As I was preparing to write this book, I continued to study the literature on leadership. And I began to notice an interesting trend toward discussions of "consciousness" and even "spirituality" in books on business leadership. One book, described as "radical and hopeful...synthesizes leading-edge thinking, firsthand knowledge, and ancient wisdom to explore the living fields that connect us to one another, to life more broadly, and, potentially, to what is 'seeking to emerge.'"[1] Another book says, "...all our lives we have been explicitly and implicitly taught to see human influence as an exercise in domination."[2] The author sends a new message, using "seed thoughts" from Jesus, Gandhi and Martin Luther King, Jr., saying that "to become a change agent, you must first change yourself and then immerse yourself in the common good, disturb the system and 'set the truth free.'"[3] If I didn't know better, I'd have thought I'd mistakenly stumbled into the philosophy or metaphysics sections of the bookstore. This simply is not the stuff you see in mainstream business books.

So, it's even more shocking to see that the books described above are anything but airy-fairy. The first is *Presence: Human Purpose and the Field of the Future*, by Peter Senge, Joseph Jaworski, C. Otto Scharmer and

Betty Sue Flowers. You might recognize Senge; he's the author of *The Fifth Discipline: The Art and Practice of the Learning Organization,* an extremely popular business management book. Jaworski is the author of the widely acclaimed book, *Synchronicity: The Inner Path of Leadership.*

These are not lightweight thinkers. Senge is senior lecturer at MIT, and has his own organization called The Society for Organizational Learning, Inc. Jaworski is co-founder of Global Leadership Initiative. Scharmer is senior lecturer at Sloan School of Management at MIT. Flowers is a former English professor at the University of Texas at Austin.

The second book I cited is *Change the World: How Ordinary People Can Accomplish Extraordinary Results,* by Robert E. Quinn. Besides being a recognized business management guru, Quinn is the M. E. Tracy Distinguished Professor of Organizational Behavior and Human Resource Management at the University of Michigan Business School.

Pretty amazing. This isn't pop-culture stuff. These are respected academics who are tapping into the idea that leadership may not exactly be about *what you do.* All of a sudden, my ideas about leadership don't seem so lonely.

Which brings me to the next obvious question: Why should you listen to *me?*

The answer starts with a story; in fact, I think it's important for you to understand that this entire book is a story. It's my story, but it's about you. (Just stay with me. You'll understand later.) It's a story with profound implications—at least, I believe so.

It's a story about how I was leading and I didn't realize it. That is, until I was given a formal position, a "leadership position." You see, I was a senior partner in a successful, multi-disciplinary, behavioral health practice, one of the largest and most productive in the Midwest. For years, I treated 30 to 40 patients a week. I was also a husband and a father and a son, a friend and a neighbor. All of these roles and relationships required me to lead.

But I never thought of myself as a leader until I became the managing partner of my firm, which put me in a formal leadership position. Suddenly, I was the guy responsible for making sure the practice was successful from a business standpoint. This was the point at which I *really* started digging into the literature on leadership. I learned my lessons well, and there was a payoff. The practice grew in every way. We had more patients, more referrals, more recognition from our peers. We added staff. We made more money. Life was good.

Then it happened: Chris, my oldest, left home for college at Purdue University. It became crystal clear to me that, although I had done all of the things psychologists tell parents to do, there was a whole bunch of things about life I'd learned in 60,000 hours of listening to patients that I hadn't thought to pass on to my own kids. Suddenly, I was the shoemaker whose own kids ran around barefoot. What to do now? Was it too late? I was distraught—and actually a little desperate. Surely, there was something I could do to give my own kids the benefit of my experience.

So, I started writing. I made a commitment to myself to write a letter to Chris and his younger sister, Julia, once a month. Each letter would address a topic I'd failed to address with the kids as they were growing up. And, I decided that—while I was at it—I might as well send the letter to my niece and nephew, Ashley and Nick (with their parents' permission, of course).

As it turned out, several of Chris's and Julia's friends requested copies of the letter, as well. Then, some of *their* friends wanted to read what I was writing. In the end, I was running a small mailing operation each month. Stories about my experiences with patients and others I'd worked with, and what I'd learned from them about life, were being read by scores of young people in high schools and colleges all over the Midwest.

And I had a revelation. I suddenly realized that *I* was a leader. I was leading in a way I'd never consciously considered before. I was leading informally every day in ways I've never really taken into account.

This alone would have been enough to convince me that I was onto something. But then I received another lesson in leadership that was far more challenging, as is often the case when life—or in this instance, death— intervenes. Steve, my friend and business partner of

twenty years, was diagnosed with multiple myeloma,
a bone cancer with no known cure.

Steve and I were closer than brothers. We'd worked
side by side for two decades. Steve was a psychiatrist and
I am a psychologist, so we teamed up to treat many of
the same patients. We were like pitcher and catcher,
a team within a team.

We were a team in the fight against cancer, too—
although Steve had the more difficult role. He beat the
cancer—*we* beat the cancer—but not the treatment.
After nearly two-and-a-half years of valiant struggle,
Steve passed away on my birthday in 2004.

My birthday. In a way, I died on that April day, too.

Steve and I were always peers. Neither of us was ever
in a formal leadership position with regard to our own
relationship. But as Steve died, I realized he had been
leading me. In his 50 years on this Earth, Steve had led
a life. He had influenced so many, including me, by how
he had lived and how he had died. It struck me that
we're all "leading a life." We're all leaders in this sense,
but few of us see ourselves as such. I know Steve didn't.

Of course, this idea of "leading a life" led me to think
about the very idea of leadership. Obviously, the word
"lead" has different meanings. The dictionary defines to
"lead" as both to "go through" and to "direct the action
of others by example." These aren't the same thing;
"experiencing" and the second as somehow "being
in charge."

In fact, however, these definitions are closer than you might imagine. We're all going through our lives, and we're all directing the action of others by the simple virtue of the fact that we're here; we exist, therefore, we lead. Your life *is* an example to someone. In some way, you're leading your spouse, your neighbors, your children, your employees, your supervisor, your parents, your friends and anyone else with whom you're in a relationship. You might not *want* to be a role model, but you *are* one, whether you want to be or not.

And I know this better than most people. Because I've spent the last 25 years sitting and listening to people from all walks of life talk about their hopes and dreams and fears and problems. And I have seen firsthand that we all lead—that we all direct the actions of others by our example.

We're all leaders. You can be a good leader or a bad leader, an enlightened leader or a dull, backward leader. You can lead people astray or you can lead them to the mountaintop. But make no mistake: *you* are a leader. And the way you lead your life will be the way you lead people in the workplace.

Even the leadership experts—the ones who are usually thinking about leadership in the more traditional sense of organizational leadership—will admit that leadership is any process of influence. This means that leadership is a process that can be exhibited by anyone, at almost any time, in almost any circumstance, almost anywhere. It also means that leadership is more about what you *are* than who you know or what position you hold, which means that leadership is more about *what* you are than *who* you are.

This last idea is so important that I want you to let it really sink in: Leadership is more about *what* you are than *who* you are. You may be a parent, a child, a friend, an employee, a boss, or all of the above. You may be John Smith or Sally Jones. All of these names and roles are tied to identity. They're the definitions you drag out and build upon when someone asks you to "tell me about yourself." But *what* you are is something deeper and more essential—and a bit more difficult to define.

So, what are you?

Isn't that the sixty-four-thousand-dollar question?

Instead of answering it, let me add a bit to the mystery: if being a leader is not about *who* you are, it's also not about *what you do*.

When you think about it, the implications of this statement are staggering. We can become pretty obsessed with "doing" in this culture; I would guess that a large percentage of my readers start (or end) their days with "to-do" lists. Most books in the self-help, management, finance and organizational leadership categories are filled with things "to do." Do this to become more physically fit. Do that to become more financially secure. Eat only potatoes if you want to lose weight. Never eat potatoes if you want to lose weight. It's all the "seven habits", the "ten rules" and the "twenty-one laws." If you follow the prescription, you'll be successful.

But all these rules are exhausting. And with each passing year, and myriad more lists of what to do and what not to do, there is also a subtle but growing sense of despair. Because we know, if we really stop to think about it, we *can't* do it all. And, even if we could, there's a sense that following all the rules wouldn't really solve our problems, anyway. As I've said, if one leadership book really has all the answers, why is everyone looking for the next one? If one diet really works, why does the next new diet book with a radically different strategy sell millions of copies, as well?

I say it's time to throw away the to-do list. I don't own any magic bullets; I don't even own a gun. If you're looking for a list of things to do to make you a better leader, you're in the wrong book.

But if you want to *be* a better leader, read on.

Just read on. You don't have to *do* anything. In our "do"-oriented culture, it's counterintuitive that, in order to do more and do better, you should "do" less. But that's exactly what I'm telling you. Do nothing! Just read and contemplate, contemplate and read. That's it! Don't do anything!

Now, I know this is difficult. It's harder to do nothing than to get about the business of doing something, anything, even if what you're doing won't work. But I'm suggesting that you do nothing. Just try it and see what happens.

And while you're about the business of doing nothing, keep in mind that I'm not asking you to *believe* anything, either.

Actually, you can't "believe" what you are about to read, at least not in the way we traditionally think of "believing." Belief is a function of something making sense; that is, information that has been subjected to your senses in a way that passes the test of logic and rationale is believable. In a way, then, believing is *about* knowledge...but it isn't knowledge itself. Believing is real, useful and sensible, but it's not all there is. In fact, it's not *most* of what there is. If you operate on what you believe alone, you are operating at a distinct disadvantage.

It would be my hope that you would subject what you read in this book—and in any book, for that matter— to the test of experience. Is what you read true in your experience or does it, over time, become truer in your experience? That's the test of "knowing" as opposed to believing. You "know" more than you'll ever believe, because knowledge is about experience; yet, many of the things you know are so integrated into your daily life that you take them for granted and barely recognize that you know them. Knowing, like breathing, is fundamental to our existence. But most of us don't even consider what it is we know unless something specific happens that brings our attention to it.

We "know", for example, love. All of us love and we all "know" we love. Love is a primary motivator of our behavior.

Much of what we do every day we do because we love;
we do all sorts of things for the people and animals and
ideas we love. But so much of the time, we are only
vaguely aware of the omnipresence of love in our lives.

Now, to make the comparison between "believing"
and "knowing", you must understand that I've never seen
love. I've seen the effects of love, but love itself is beyond
my perception. Therefore, to talk about "believing" in
love—not in the power of love or the value of love, but in
love itself—seems a little silly.

But I do "know" love. I've experienced love. And
though I'd be hard pressed to "prove" love to someone
who wanted it objectified so they could believe it, I have
no doubt of its importance in my life. Love is fundamental
yet invisible, palpable yet immeasurable, essential yet
unmanageable, "knowable" yet "unbelievable."

And, to illustrate my point about taking the things we
know for granted, how many times have you heard someone
bemoan the loss of a love that didn't seem all that special
until it was gone? (Perhaps you've experienced this
yourself. Most of us have, in one way or another.)
Love was there all the time, right there in front of us.
We "knew" it. But we forgot that we knew. As Willie
Nelson sings, "Little things I should have said and done,
I just never took the time. But you were always on my
mind." That's why it's so important to *remember to remember*
the things we know. Because, ultimately, knowing is about
wisdom; wisdom is knowledge remembered.

Albert Einstein said that the true art of questioning is not to discover what one does not know and, therefore, must be taught, but to discover what one *knows*.[4] We learn so many things we never have to consider; yet we *know* so many things we may never consider at all. I hope that, as you read, you're reminded of a few of the things you know.

It's already starting to feel a little airy-fairy, isn't it? Don't say I didn't warn you.

And there's nothing wrong with a little skepticism. It's healthy and normal.

And speaking of what you "know", I have a question for you: Which would be a worse situation for you—believing something that turned out to be untrue, or refusing to believe something that turned out to be true? In other words, would you rather risk being thought of as gullible, or cynical?

None of us wants to be thought of as gullible. We all want to think we can see through scams, that we won't be taken in by three-card monte games or boiler-room schemes or the promises of our children that they'll really, really get their homework done if we just let them go to the concert on a school night. If you're gullible, it means you're intellectually lazy. That's the only way all of these little old ladies can fall for the Canadian Lottery scam—you know, the one where the nice man calls and tells them they're going to win a million dollars if they'll just send a check for fifty thousand dollars to cover the taxes. You're too smart for that. It could never happen to you.

Cynicism, on the other hand, is almost fashionable. It's a natural consequence of our "prove-it-or-I-don't-believe-it" society, and it shows up in all sorts of ways. Cynicism is at least a kissing cousin of the style of comedy that has been popular for several decades: not the outsider comedy of the Marx Brothers and Monty Python, but the insider comedy of David Letterman and Bill Maher. These guys aren't silly. They're smart, cool, hip. They know everything. And if you're not with them and all the other comedians and culture critics and political pundits who jam the airwaves these days—if you are not doubting or critical of the motives of others—then you're not sophisticated or intelligent.

This cynical approach to everyday life has its rewards. If you're a cynic, you get to be smart and hip. And this would be fine if not for the devastating effects of cynical living.

Beyond all the sarcasm and fun, cynicism is really a contemptuous distrust of human behavior as being primarily self-serving, which is an awfully ugly way to view the world...not that it isn't understandable. Cynicism is actually born of the experience of disappointment in past relationships, arrogance in present relationships or fear of disappointment in future relationships. In other words, cynicism is born of the experience and expectation of the worst.

And we've all experienced the worst in people. We've all trusted people and had our trust betrayed, usually by the people closest to us: our spouses and parents and children and partners and best friends. That's the way people are, after all: even the best intentioned among us have let others down. So, isn't it better to be wary so we don't continue to get hurt?

Well...no. The problem with cynicism is that it's emotionally and physically unhealthy. It's long been understood that people who have a negative attitude have poor-quality relationships and are more prone to melancholy. This would seem to make sense. But there's also evidence that people who are cynical are more susceptible to infectious conditions such as influenza and colds. Even more disconcerting is the suggestion that this negativity in relationships may contribute to an increased likelihood of more serious and life-threatening conditions such as cancer and heart disease. And cynicism has been shown to be related to shortened lifespan.[5]

So, if your approach to this book is negative—if you are cynical about me or what I am saying—I request only that you pause for a moment, take a deep breath, open your mind and consider a more hopeful approach. There is nothing to fear here. I'm not asking you to accept or believe me or anything that you don't already "know."

Also: Don't expect a particularly straight line from here to the leadership lessons you hope to take from this book. We're going to go around a few bends and duck into a couple of blind alleys along the way. It's going to be an interesting ride, I promise you. If you think you've veered off course, stay with it: I think it will all make sense in the end.

The next section, "Awakening to the Power Within", gives you the background and the perspective you need to get the most out of the book. It's filled with ideas and theories about leadership, the state of business today, why certain management strategies work and don't work, and the problems with traditional views of leadership. At the end of this section, I discuss the idea of an underlying reality that is mostly unseen—and that may challenge your notions of common sense. That's because this reality is all about *uncommon sense.*

And that's the subject of the bulk of this book: The Six Universal Principles of Uncommon Sense. You certainly know some of these principles. Some of them you may even believe. But until you really examine how they work in your life, you'll never be the most effective leader you can be.

Finally, please bear in mind that this is not another leadership book, but rather a book on leading. "Leadership" is a role or a function. "Leading" is an action. If you're more interested in the idea of leadership, by all means, continue to read the current leadership literature. If you want to lead, I think you'll find some valuable insights here. In either case, to be sure you're becoming the leader you really want to be, occasionally ask yourself, "how's this working for me?"

PART I:
AWAKENING TO
THE POWER WITHIN

What Do You Mean, *"Leadership"*?

One of the interesting things about most leadership books is that they rarely define what they're about; that is, they assume we all understand what we mean when we talk about "leadership." You may have an intuitive idea about leadership, but most people have never actually taken the time to consciously think about what leadership *is*.

So, that's where we're going to start. In academic circles, leadership is traditionally thought to be a function of two variables: competence of the leader and power. Let's take a look at these variables one at a time.

Leadership competence, often referred to as the "task behaviors" of leadership, is the focus of most leadership training. One reason is that it's the sort of thing you can actually *do* something about: you can make lists of skills and techniques and train people to implement your ideas about what leaders should do.

This type of leadership, that emphasizes the competency of the leader, is called *transactional leadership.*[6] It's called transactional leadership because it involves the exchange of rewards for compliance with the leader's directives; in other words, you, the leader, gain followers by exchanging rewards and benefits for their loyalty. (The flip side, of course, is that followers receive punishment, or at least no benefit, when they don't comply.) Transactional leadership appeals to the employee's self-interest, and works best when what needs doing is relatively straightforward or routine, because its focus is on getting things done.

As you might imagine, then, transactional leadership training is all about doing things. Every year, employers spend billions of dollars to improve leadership competency, focusing on such skills as communication, time management, project management, strategic planning, problem solving and conflict management, right hiring, and motivation. And not just employers—individual spending on leadership competency is in the billions, as well. Parents attend parenting workshops. Couples go to weekend marriage retreats. People buy books and CDs and videos and go to counseling, all to gain a better understanding of the skills and techniques they think they need to be more competent in the life they are leading.

So, how are we to square all of this effort to become better leaders with the idea that leadership is *really* about some sort of personal charisma? Because, historically, it was thought that leadership was more a function of personal characteristics of the leader than the things the leader did—something they were born with, as opposed to something that could be learned. This was the "great-person" view of leadership. In a way, it was focused on competency, too, but this competency was thought to be more innate, less something you could learn in a book or a seminar. The personal characteristics that made for great leaders included intelligence, verbal skills, physical size or attractiveness, dominance, personability and even the quality of the leader's education. Leaders went to Harvard. Followers went to community college.

The great-person view of leadership may have taken a back seat to transactional leadership today, but it certainly hasn't gone away. Our culture still emphasizes the power of personality. I'm sure you can think of several people who seem to be famous—not because of anything they've done, but just because they have a certain *je ne sais quoi*—and charisma is still thought to be a key aspect of leadership. Great-person leaders have charisma, a strong need for power, a high level of self-confidence and intense belief in their own ideas.[7] Charisma is related to temperament and is not a characteristic that can be learned.

So, traditionally, leadership has been considered to be a combination of inherent characteristics that an individual leader has, such as charisma, and a set of skills that can be learned and developed, such as communication skills or strategic planning. And it's true: Leaders with a high degree of personal appeal combined with intelligence, experience and the ability to communicate, are gifted and often demonstrate remarkable effectiveness—especially in the short term and in impersonal leadership. But the human landscape is littered with examples of these people who, over the long run, have shown themselves to be ineffective in leading a life. They may make money and accumulate all the outward trappings of success, but, ultimately, they inspire very few.

An AMERICAN *Success Story*

Dave was a business leader who had succeeded in all of the usual ways that we, in our culture, measure success. He'd risen through the ranks of a major corporation and shown remarkable savvy in anticipating market trends. He was considered a money-making genius because of his remarkable leadership competence.

Yet, Dave was miserable. At age sixty, he was in poor physical health. As he grew older, he realized he had become increasingly isolated. Most of the people who had been his closest companions had little use for him. In addition to his advancing age and fading health, his competence in the marketplace began to decline. People around him envied his money, but no one admired him. These people seemed interested in what Dave could "do" and, specifically, what he could do for them—his competence—but few would ever consider having more than a business dinner with him. As his professional skills faded and his advice became suspect, even his business dinners became more and more sporadic.

Some might suggest that Dave had it coming. For years, he'd been primarily interested in people who could somehow do something for him. Given the choice between arranging a late meeting or attending his son's baseball game, Dave routinely chose the meeting. "After all," he would rationalize, "I'm making a living for my family. I'm preparing for the future of my family. The meeting is really more important for my family."

Dave's consistent dedication to his job early in his career created new opportunities. In fact, he had the chance on his way up to take what he considered his dream job, but doing so would require relocating to another part of the country—something his wife and kids had no interest in doing. Dave took the promotion and made the move anyway, opting for professional success over sensitivity to his family's desires. Naturally, this decision caused even more fractures in Dave's fragile family relationships.

How many people do you know like Dave? How many "leaders" like Dave have our culture of leadership competence produced: leaders who know how to make money, but don't know how to have meaningful relationships? I suspect—actually, I know—that leaders like Dave have not only unsatisfying personal relationships, but also short-term, shallow and unsatisfying business relationships, as well. They don't inspire loyalty. They don't hang onto employees. They see other people as means to an end, so others treat leaders like Dave the same way in return.

And so, Dave ends up lonely, bitter, sick and afraid. Is it any wonder?

Donut Leaders

Less emphasized than leadership competence is an equally important aspect of leadership: the power of the leader in leading. Although often overlooked, this aspect of leadership is what actually makes the difference between a leader who manages a life and a leader who leads a life.

I recently had a discussion about leadership competence and leadership power with Frank, a successful business leader. I explained to him that most efforts to improve leadership in an organization are aimed at the competency issues, and that tends to create leaders of skill, but with limited power.

Frank pulled out his pen, grabbed a sheet of paper, and drew two concentric circles. His drawing looked like a donut. He said, "It seems to me that you're saying most leadership training is directed at the space between the two circles, but not much training is focused on the space in the center." The space between the circles, the donut, is the stuff of being competent. But the center, the donut hole, represents what the leader is, the leader's power. Frank suggested that truly powerful, effective leaders have no hole in their leadership donut.

DONUT LEADERS

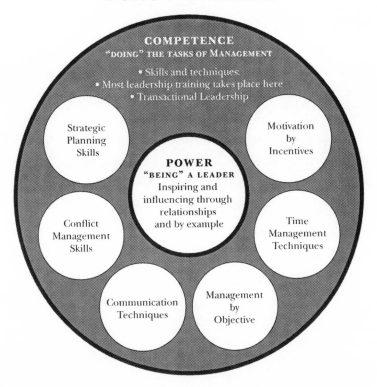

The Donut Leader is Missing Something—
The Power of Influence and Benefit from Their Competence

"By focusing on leadership competence, we're creating hollow leaders, people with nothing on the inside," he said.

He's right—and this tendency to create hollow leaders is affecting business in a big way. It has been estimated that the current competency-focused style of leadership in this country is costing us half of the human potential available.[8] This certainly is not due to lack of skill, or lack of money spent on trying to gain skills, but rather to a lack of effectiveness and power in the application of leadership skills.

With so little effort directed at filling the "donut hole", we are left with "donut" leaders. These are people who know how to *do* leadership, but aren't *being* leaders. They have the skills. They're technically sound. But they're not very powerful leaders because there's nothing at the center. They're skilled at completing tasks and solving problems. But can they, as a result of what they are as people, inspire their charges to become more than they ever thought they could be?

LEADERSHIP
Power

It has been my observation over the past quarter-century that leadership power—recently defined as "the capacity and ability to lead"[9]—is what makes a leader more or less effective in any type of leadership situation. The greater a leader's power, the greater his or her potential for influencing others—for being a truly effective leader.

So, what is an effective leader? In business, an effective leader is someone who helps other people accomplish more than they would if there had been no such leadership. The effective leader must maximize the company's assets, and since the most valuable assets in this information-driven economy lie in the heads of the employees, the most effective leaders ultimately engage the hearts and minds of employees and inspire them to participate in accomplishing the important tasks at hand. Employees who follow powerful leaders find that they can be true to themselves. They're better able to use their inherent talents and strengths, and, as a consequence, achieve more together than they would have alone. The job gets done through the "flow" of coworkers, rather than command and control of traditional management.

At home, effective leadership may inspire a loving, rewarding family life. But whether at work or at home, while accomplishment is important, leadership is more about the *way* things are accomplished than the accomplishments themselves. The "how" of the accomplishment is the point of leadership power. Open, willing, flowing participation, rather than begrudging effort, is the goal.

Truly powerful leaders know how to inspire people to go beyond what they would have done if left to their own devices. On the other hand, lots of leaders are leaders in name only. They have leadership titles and responsibilities, but don't inspire confidence or motivate people to do more.

This leads to the inarguable conclusion that leadership power is, at least in part, a function of "internal social capital"[10]; in layman's terms, that means how much trust there is between the leader and those being led. Leading and following are, after all, personal. They are experiential and cannot be assumed. The better the experience, the more engaged the follower. The more engaged the follower, the greater the effort and the more committed the follower.

And according to recent reports, 76 percent of employees are only moderately engaged[11]—and their level of engagement is declining[12]. Think about it: *three-quarters* of employees don't really care very much about what they're doing. This startling fact suggests that the key to successful leading lies in reaching not the 11 percent of followers who are highly engaged or the 13 percent who are disaffected, but the 76 percent who are only moderately engaged. To tap into the potential of this moderately engaged, semi-motivated group makes all the difference in any organization.

What's the key to tapping that potential? It's not any technique or style of management. It's simply the *power of the leader to lead*. According to studies, employees say that their leaders have 50 to 70 percent of the influence over their work teams' performance.[13] Particularly powerful leaders can exert up to 90 percent influence. Of course, this influence isn't necessarily positive. The leader has the capacity to demoralize, as well as to encourage and motivate. To paraphrase author Marcus Buckingham, people don't leave companies, they leave managers.[14]

The power of the leader to lead hinges on trust. Trust, not time sheets or incentive plans or Six Sigma initiatives, turns out to be the key to increased productivity.

Transformational *Leaders*

Over the past 25 years, I've worked with lots of people who would be considered leaders in their fields and in their individual companies. And I can tell you this: a leader's effectiveness doesn't necessarily correlate with his or her level of training. I've worked with highly trained CEOs who were extremely competent, but whose effectiveness paled when compared with CEOs of similar talent who had tapped some sort of power within.

Likewise, on the home front, I've been party to hours and hours of "strategy discussions" about parenting techniques with adolescents, and I've come to the conclusion that they invariably miss the mark. I've seen teens thrive under the reign of conservative, strict parents. I've also seen them wilt—or rebel. I've seen the same extremes with the kids of liberal, permissive parents.

I've quit believing that, when it comes to providing leadership as a parent, strategy matters much at all. It's important that you *have* a strategy, because a lack of consistency is poor parenting. But regardless of whether you are very strict or very permissive or somewhere in between, what really makes the difference is the quality of the parent's relationship with the teen. Successful parenting seems to be more about *what you are* as a parent, not *what you do* as a parent.

Of course, you still have to have leadership competence. But when leaders in any setting are competent and also understand and embrace this power within, they have the capacity to transform their relationships—and often help transform the people they're leading. These leaders have power that is beyond position or authority. Their effectiveness starts with their competence—in their knowing what to do as leaders. But there is that intangible element that makes them and the people influenced by them more effective than would be expected, based on their skills and techniques alone.

This phenomenon is called *transformational leadership.* The influence a transformational leader can have is inspirational, not because the leader is a cheerleader or only because the leader is competent, but, most importantly, because the leader can be *trusted.* It comes from within; it's based on the person, on the relationships with those they lead, and not position, leverage or charisma.

You can think of transformational leaders. Transformational leaders are like the quarterback who, while certainly physically capable at his trade, is not the most talented quarterback in the league. And, while he is surrounded by competent athletes, his team is not the most talented in the league. Yet, time and again, his team rises to the occasion, driving the length of the field in the closing seconds of big games to score and beat more talented teams. Think of Joe Montana, a gifted leader with middling quarterback skills, versus Dan Marino, an all-world athlete who never managed to lead his team to a Super Bowl victory. More than transacting plays and "playing" the game, quarterbacks like Montana transform their teammates and their teams into more than they really are in terms of mere competence. Their leadership ability is beyond competence; intangible, yet undeniable.

Transactional leaders, we may envy. Transformational leaders, we admire.

"Be *All* That YOU Can *Be*"

One of the immutable laws of the universe is the speed of light: 186,000 miles per second. Nothing can exceed the speed of light—it's the upper limit of speed—and the speed of light is always exactly 186,000 miles per second. It's the "C", or "constant", in Einstein's famous equation $E=MC^2$.

Speaking of upper limits, can you be more intelligent than your true intellectual capability allows? Of course not! At any given point in your life, you have a given intellectual capacity, and you can't exceed that capacity, not even temporarily. You can perform *below* your abilities, but not above; if you're not Einstein, you never will be. The best you can do is perform *at* capacity.

Now, if you study and learn and work hard, you can modestly raise your intelligence relative to your peers. But there is still a limitation as to how much you can raise your intellectual performance. You still have a capacity you can't exceed.

One way to think about using your intelligence is to discover and work within your areas of intellectual strength. In their book, *Now, Discover Your Strengths*, Marcus Buckingham and Donald Clifton say that "the real tragedy in life is not that each of us doesn't have enough strengths, it's that we fail to use the ones we have."[15] They go on to talk about how, instead of focusing on your weaknesses, you need to discover your areas of strength and work to develop them.

Buckingham and Clifton are talking about strengths— your talents and proclivities. You certainly do have these—some of us are good at math, some of us are good at writing, some of us are good with our hands— and you may be happier and more productive if you focus your energy on them.

But I'm saying something else: *You already have everything you need to be everything you need to be.* You already have the power within. I'm not talking about strengths or interests, but a power that lies at the center of your being that makes *everything* you do and everything you have—both strengths and weaknesses—more powerful. It's true: Even in your weaknesses, there is great power to lead your life and lead others.

The problem is that most of us don't tap into this power.

But the point at which you engage the power within, a point at which you "see" things differently, is where you can begin *being* the leader you can be. Your ability to lead others is more than a set of behaviors and competencies that you can learn. It's certainly about having competence. But leading a whole life and effectively leading others is more about discovering the innate power that lies within. Like the speed of light, it's a constant. Like relativity, it's a bit of an elusive concept. Fortunately, though, you don't have to be a genius to discover it.

MANAGING *& Leading*

Over time and across the spectrum of literature on the subject, much has been made of the difference between management and leadership. It has been said that "managers do things right and leaders do the right things." This is a valid distinction, and suggests that the difference between a manager and a leader is primarily one of perspective. I agree—but would add that great leaders have discovered a powerful new vision of life that lies within, and therefore are effective as both managers and leaders.

But what is "managing", and what can we manage? In truth, we can manage only one thing: the completion of tasks. And when it comes to completing tasks, you can really manage only one person: yourself.

To some, these assertions may seem obvious. You can "make" yourself do something, but you can't really make anyone else do anything they don't want to do. You can influence and barter and threaten and wheedle, but you can't make them. Prisoners of war endure all sorts of horrible torture, even to the point of death. You can't *make* anyone do anything.

And yet, there is a natural human tendency, related to ego, to continue to believe we can manage others. After all, we create management structures. We call people managers and have managers' meetings. Managers *think* they manage people; it's what they're paid to do. You may think you manage people, but it's only an illusion. Don't believe it!

Middle managers have a particularly difficult time coming to understand the fact that they can't really manage people. For the most part, middle managers have been promoted to middle management because they are task-competent. It's assumed that they should be able to lead others in the completion of tasks as competently as they are able to manage themselves. Inevitably, this leads to problems when this task-completing ability doesn't translate to getting others to complete tasks.

And so, many middle managers attempt to micromanage and are met with frustration. They lose trust in the people they manage. They can't do everything themselves and they can't rely on anyone else, so they feel out of control. Consequently, they try to muscle others into doing things their way, which is met with resistance, either passive or direct or both. Trust breaks down. Hostility grows within people throughout the organization and spreads into active conflict.

And what happens to the poor middle manager? What becomes of this person who was so good at what she did that she was promoted and put in charge of others to manage their work? According to one study, the consequences include social isolation, illness and even premature death.[16]

It's a supreme frustration to be charged with managing people when you can really only manage yourself. We can manage only ourselves and the tasks we're responsible for, nothing more and nothing less. No one manages anyone else.

Leadership—that's a different story. We *can* lead. Even so, the people we lead do only what they decide to do, not what they're told to do. Every parent with a child beyond a week or so old knows this.

In order to keep their positions and their paychecks, people will do what's required of them. But to give extra effort—to go above and beyond—they must be led. And that's not a problem. People actually yearn to be led. In being led, they want to be inspired. Inspiration is at the heart of influencing others. Followers crave to be influenced. They actually want to be inspired to do their best.

That's what the leader has to do. To get the best effort out of their followers, leaders must persuade them to participate enthusiastically in their work. This participation, remember, is voluntary and given only when people are inspired and willing to be influenced by a leader who has them engaged and committed.

Finally, others will follow only if the leader has credibility—that is, if the leader is competent and trust-worthy. If followers find their leader to have credibility, they'll be much more willing to accomplish the tasks that must be completed. Think about your own experience with parents, teachers, mentors, supervisors and friends. How much effort do you give if you think someone leading you can't be trusted, or isn't worthy of your respect? Isn't this, after all, why teenagers rebel? They've reached a point in their young lives where they (most often mistakenly) believe they know more than their parents.

In any case, to manage the completion of tasks that are beyond our ability, we must engage the cooperation of others. We have to influence others to give extra effort; that is, we have to find some way of getting people to want to do their jobs, and do them well. This extra effort is up to the follower's discretion, and thus is known as *discretionary effort.*[17]

The *Difference* is *All* in Their HEADS

Discretionary effort is a concept that has been around since the 1930s, but, even today, business leaders are unfamiliar with the term or its meaning—and parents, those intrepid leaders on the home front, nearly never apply this concept to their leadership responsibilities.

And, make no mistake: there's *a lot* of discretionary effort available. Surveys of American workers consistently show that employees estimate that they give roughly 50 percent of their full capacity in order to get a paycheck.[18] Anything they give beyond 50 percent of their capacity is discretionary: they decide whether to give the extra effort.

No doubt, you've had this experience of giving discretionary effort. Even the most diligent workers among us have toiled at jobs where the leadership was uninspiring at best and demoralizing at worse. As a consequence, we gave "an honest day's work for an honest day's pay", but nothing more.

On the other hand, I hope you've also had the experience of working with or for someone who inspired you to be more than you ever knew you could be. For this kind of leader, you were willing to go well beyond the minimum effort. You did your honest day's work and then some, offering effort beyond that for which you were being paid. You did it willingly and gladly; in fact, it made you feel great.

The U.S. Department of Labor reports that "better leadership"—again, the sort of leadership I've been referring to as transformational leadership—results in greater productivity. You can see how this meshes with the concept of discretionary effort. Of course, those companies with transformational leaders would have greater productivity. It only stands to reason. (It's easy to see transformational leadership in the family environment, too. Some parents get routine, required effort from their kids. Some parents get more.)

One of my clients is Alice, the CEO of a small manu-
facturing company. This company makes a product that
is something of a commodity: many other companies
produce essentially the same thing. Alice told me that,
as the industry has matured, her traditional market edge
has evaporated. "I use the same equipment. I buy the
same raw materials at approximately the same prices.
I even hire many of the same people, because they move
around within the industry. So where is my advantage?"
she asked.

I would maintain that her advantage lies in her ability
to tap discretionary effort.

If she and her competition are all moving roughly the
same amount of product (and, in fact, they are), then—
all other things being equal—if she can get 25 percent
discretionary effort on top of the 50% that everyone
already gets, she'll need one-third fewer employees to get
the same job done. Alice's company would save millions
of dollars in wages and benefits that her competitors have
to pay to do the same job—to say nothing of the increase
in customer satisfaction and loyalty due to improved
employee morale. So, if you think better leadership can't
have direct impact on the bottom line, think again.

This case involving Alice's company is a clear example
of the need for leaders to understand that people truly
are their most valuable assets—and that maximizing the
organization's potential means dealing with those assets
most effectively. In the Industrial Age, the assets that had

to be maximized were usually hard assets, such as bricks, mortar and machines. But in today's Information Age, the greatest assets any employer has are his employees' knowledge and willingness to expend discretionary effort. You might say that the difference is all in their heads.

Times They ARE *a-Changing*

If you don't believe that times are changing, consider the value of Google in 2006 versus the value of General Motors. Could you have imagined 10 years ago that the value of a little search engine company could even come within a sniff of an industrial giant? GM has been in business many times longer. GM has many, many more hard assets. But value on the stock market seems unrelated to either of these factors.

In the Information Age, change happens fast. It took 100 years, the whole of the nineteenth century, for information to double once. It now doubles approximately every year. That's breathtaking.

And the speed of change means we have to change the way we operate. For example, the concept of conquest and control is growing obsolete. There's just too much

information to continue to micromanage anything.
In our own lives with our partners, spouses, kids, friends,
employees, supervisors, parents, anyone we relate to, we
have to let go of the desire to micromanage. Every time
you think you get your arms around a problem, it's moved.

Consider that, even in a hard science such as physics,
the introduction of quantum theory is leading away from
the usual reductionism to an awareness that there's always
more unseen than seen. Reductionism is just too simplistic.

And as information is exploding and becoming more
complicated, the world is shrinking. A shrinking world
necessitates an increased emphasis on tolerance.
No longer can we be concerned about only "our kind",
but rather we must develop a greater sense of community
and include "all kinds." Again, this is an effect of the
Information Age. We can't be concerned only with our
tribe or our neighborhood or even our nation or our
continent or our planet.

You might think all of this information would be
empowering—and, for a while it is. But the mountains
of data we're expected to deal with and the rapidity of
change too often become immobilizing. It's a curious
function of too much too fast. Choice represents freedom
until there are too many choices too quickly. How many
brands of chocolate chip cookies do you need to consider? What's the very best kind of shampoo for your hair?
What's exactly the right color and style of carpet for
your bedroom?

In the face of all this complexity, change, speed and crisis, to believe that we can lead as we always have is to set ourselves up for powerlessness and failure. That's why we must tap into power of a different kind, at a different level, for a different age. In this information-based economy, intellectual capital is the most appreciable asset. Great leadership maximizes this asset to reach the organization's potential.

And one of the scariest things for employers is that their companies' greatest assets are so mobile. Employee retention is a critical issue for every company. How do you keep the organization's greatest assets so inspired and motivated and happy that they won't walk away? This is the leader's challenge.

THEORY *X* VS. THEORY *y*

Whether you're conscious of it or not, your management or leadership style is the result of some theory or philosophy of human behavior. And it probably falls into one of two camps: Theory X or Theory Y.

Traditional models of behavior have assumed that followers dislike work and will avoid it. This philosophy proposes that most people really want someone to tell them what to do—which is where the belief that followers must be coerced, controlled, directed and threatened comes from.

This theory of behavior is known in psychology circles as Theory X.[19] According to Theory X, people are naturally irresponsible and without ambition. This leads naturally to the traditional, Industrial Age, control-oriented management approach that actually encourages followers to be dependent on supervisors— and the greater the dependency, the greater the leverage for coercion.

Now, here's the shocking part: Theory X is true.

But Theory X is not true because of the way people really *are*, but because of the way they're *managed*; it's an effect, rather than a cause. People *do* lack motivation and initiative when they are controlled and threatened, and it seems that only more control will get them to straighten up and fly right. It's a self-perpetuating cycle—and the result of a flawed and unsophisticated understanding of human motivation.

The alternative leadership philosophy is referred to as Theory Y. Theory Y recognizes that all people have needs, and that those needs have an inherent hierarchy. All behavior is motivated by unsatisfied needs; therefore, the great leader looks for and seeks to fulfill the unsatisfied needs of those she leads. And as long as the basic needs of food and clothing and shelter and security have been addressed, most people today actually need to belong, to feel valued and to achieve.

A truly powerful leader sees followers as having knowledge and skills that she, herself, lacks. She recognizes that followers are motivated to apply their knowledge and skills most effectively and efficiently through discretionary effort. In fact, the organization's desired productivity and profitability can be achieved *only* through the application of discretionary effort.[20]

And make no mistake: you can't have one philosophy of leading at work and another at home. It may appear that you can, at least for a while. But, sooner or later, being a Theory X boss and a Theory Y husband and father catches up with you. I've worked with thousands of men and women in the past 25 years, and my experience is consistent: you'll always regress to the lowest common denominator. In other words, if you view your followers as a means to an end, you'll end up, like it or not, treating your kids, wife, neighbors and friends that way, too.

It all has to do with your level of awareness to the needs of others. If you have no sensitivity to the personal needs of those who work with you, you are inevitably blind and insensitive to those who love you. Inevitably! I've never seen an exception.

LEADING WITH *Fear*

Why is it that so many leaders resort to tactics designed to manipulate and control their followers? Why do they think they can use fear to motivate? What is it that's so seductive about Theory X?

It all goes back to basic human needs. In the Industrial Age, when there was a strict hierarchy in companies, churches and even families, authority was feared. Our most basic needs are physiological—and it was possible, even within the last 100 years, to manipulate employees with the threat that they'd lose their jobs and not be able to feed their families, even that very day.

It's still that way in parts of the world—in much too much of the world. But most of us in the United States don't live with that fear today. Most of us are going to eat today whether or not we're employed. That's a good thing, for many reasons—including the fact that trying to lead people through manipulation based on the threat of unsatisfied physiological need is empty and ineffective.

After physiological needs are satisfied, people next seek safety. The threat of harm is a powerful motivator. Of course, physically striking someone as a management tactic has been disallowed long ago by the laws of civilized society. Even in families, parents have developed more humane and effective strategies for dealing with their kids than inflicting physical pain.

But old habits die hard. Even though physiological and physical threats are no longer realistic, fear-based management techniques are still popular. Too many leaders continue to use punitive techniques to get their followers to do what they want them to do.

Consider:

Many parents still spank their children, threaten physical violence and use systems of punishment to try to curb bad behavior. In fact, there seems even to be a growing trend toward "tougher" parenting based on the idea that permissiveness has exacerbated societal ills from crime to drug abuse to teen pregnancy.

State lawmakers continue to promote the death penalty as a deterrent to violent crime, even though there is no evidence that it has any such effect.

Some religions hold the threat of eternal punishment over the heads of humankind for wrong behavior or for failing to believe the "right" things without fully appreciating and embracing the saving presence of grace in every moment of every day.

And this is all to say nothing of the coercive, manipulative, threatening bosses most of us have experienced (and some of us have been) in the workplace.

And it would be one thing if this sort of fear-based leadership technique worked. But its effectiveness is limited. At best, it works in the short term. And it works only part of the time. Because you have to actually force people into compliance, this approach never works when you're not around to keep up the pressure. Again— you've probably experienced a work situation in which everyone looks busy when the manager's around, but all the work stops and the complaining begins when the manager's out of the room.

Curiously, even the most sophisticated management techniques, such as Total Quality Management, don't work in the presence of fear. Without a sense of safety, people are more focused on self-protection than on organizational interests.[21] All great leaders, whether at home, in the community or at work, must provide and encourage safety if they are going to be truly effective.

So, if threats and fear don't really work to motivate people, what *does* work? Well, because of our society's ability to meet most immediate physiological needs and our relative freedom from physical threat, we are left with a beautiful opportunity to move to a higher level of need. The next levels of human need are belongingness, followed by the desire to achieve.[22] When we know we'll eat today, and we're relatively assured that we won't be abused, we next want to belong and to accomplish. These become our primary motivating factors.

Which means that real leadership, transformational leadership, understands, considers and taps into these powerful human needs.

WHAT DO THE
Data Say?

The idea of tapping into people's needs for belonging and achievement is all well and good, you might say, but does it work? Is it just the milquetoast idea of some fuzzy-brained psychologist, or does this stuff actually work in the real world?

It actually works.

Remember our discussion of discretionary effort? Studies have shown that, as a general rule, the greater the voluntary actions of followers toward the leader's intended direction, the more powerful and effective the leadership. Being a great leader means that people follow you willingly.

When people follow you willingly and have their needs for belonging and achievement met, they tend to hang around. There's simply less employee turnover in organizations where Theory Y is the dominant leadership philosophy. Having talented, motivated and committed employees is not only the best productivity strategy, but also the best employee retention strategy an organization can have.[23]

With greater employee retention, several things happen. First, better employee retention is accompanied by better employee attendance. Second, better employee retention and attendance are, not surprisingly, related to better productivity. But did you know that better employee retention is the largest contributing variable to better customer service?[24] And it follows that better customer service is related to greater customer satisfaction and customer retention. When you lead with competence and power, employees work harder, smarter and are more committed. Companies that understand their employees are their most important strategic asset experience levels of productivity up to 40 percent higher than their Theory X competitors.[25]

And what about profitability? Well, hiring and rehiring are expensive. So is absenteeism. So is customer turnover. Interestingly, an increase of as little as five percent in customer retention has been shown to increase profits by 25 to 95 percent.[26] So, employee satisfaction leads to employee retention leads to customer retention, which drops straight to the bottom line.

And there's more: there's even evidence that Theory Y-oriented companies have lower overhead because there is less need for management when employees are fulfilled in their jobs.[27] They actually do a better job of managing themselves. On many occasions, I've witnessed how employees work smarter when they're engaged and inspired by their leaders. More loyalty and less fear promote a willingness, even a desire, to find better ways of doing things.

So with less turnover, better attendance, more diligent effort and thinking employees who require less management, is it any wonder that Theory Y-oriented companies have up to 50 percent greater profitability?[28] That's correct—50 percent across industries and economic conditions.[29]

This is obviously more than just the theory of an old headshrinker. This is so very practical!

The RULE of
One-Eighth

In spite of the fact that Theory Y makes sense psychologically and intuitively, and that there are data to support the importance of people as the strategy for a more productive and more profitable business, most businesspeople aren't paying attention. Only 12.5 percent of companies in any given industry actually apply Theory Y and harness its potential. This curious phenomenon is called the *Rule of One-Eighth,* and understanding it is a clear market advantage.[30]

According to the Rule of One-Eighth, lots of companies are aware of the importance of people as their key strategy; yet, half do nothing to further engage employees. Of the remaining half, another half applies at least one technique for a brief period, but then stops. That leaves a quarter of the original group—half of which applies a comprehensive program to engage employees, but won't sustain the effort long enough to realize the benefits in productivity or profitability. This leaves one-eighth, or 12.5 percent, of companies in any industry that benefit from the people-as-strategy approach.

Why would any company in this highly competitive business environment not take advantage of this clear benefit? In a word: fear. Fear inhibits the ability to turn knowledge, even the knowledge of how to have a clear competitive advantage, into the necessary ingredients for a more efficient and effective company. Fear results in short-term thinking and focuses employees' attention on the individual, rather than collective, good. Fear keeps leaders from seeing people as their most effective strategy. Most companies simply follow the majority and willingly forfeit market advantage for safety.

How you engage people in the process of work and bring about a more effective, efficient and profitable work environment is partially a function of competency, but mostly the consequence of the power of the leadership. Your competitors can hire equally talented employees. Your real market advantage has to go beyond talent and skill. And real power in any setting is always a function of what the leader *is* more than position, authority, talent or what the leader *knows*. It's not slogans. It's not productivity programs. It's the direct result of people seeing who the leader is and how the leader behaves and how the leader manages himself. It's inspiration by example.

It's the power within.

Managing to LEAD *and* Leading to MANAGE

So, how do you become a leader of not only competence but also power? Perhaps a brief recap is in order:

You can really manage only yourself and your own tasks. If you're charged with managing tasks you can't complete yourself—and, in at least some way, most of us are—you have to lead others, which means you have to understand how to lead them. After all, others do what they decide to do, not what they're told, and therefore must *decide* to follow you. Theory X—that is, manipulating and controlling others—is ill-suited for motivating people today (and inhumane, even if it did work). Theory Y says people need to belong and achieve, and that's how you motivate them. People follow leaders they trust; in order to be trusted, you must be trustworthy.

And, perhaps as a part of our survival instinct, we don't trust people who are concerned only with themselves or those who are interested in only what they want right now. Followers, whether they're our employees or our kids, are keen observers of their leaders' behavior. As followers, we do place great faith in people who have interest in the greater good and seem to have that uncanny sense of what's best in the long run. With these leaders, we're willing to take risk, to try a little harder, to give more because we feel safe that we're not being exploited and we desire to be a part of something bigger than any one of us.

So, why should anyone trust you? Why should anyone follow you? Why should anyone give more than the minimum needed to keep getting a paycheck? Do the people who follow you honestly believe that you have their backs? Or, are you simply using them to get stuff done and further your own career?

Hot Air

One morning, a man took off in a hot air balloon. He had a lunch appointment across town, and planned to balloon to the restaurant. A couple of hours went by before the man realized he didn't recognize anything below him. He was lost.

So, the man in a balloon reduced altitude and, before too long, he spotted a woman working in her yard. He descended a bit more and shouted, "Excuse me, can you help me? I promised a friend I would meet him an hour ago, but I don't know where I am!"

The woman replied, "You're in a hot air balloon hovering approximately 30 feet above the ground. You're between 40 and 41 degrees north latitude and between 59 and 60 degrees west longitude."

"You must be an engineer," said the balloonist.

"I am," replied the woman, "How did you know?"

"Well," answered the man, "everything you told me is technically correct, but I've no idea what to make of your information, and, the fact is, I'm still lost. Frankly, you've not been much help at all. If anything, you've delayed my trip."

The woman below responded, "Well then, you must be in management."

"I am," replied the balloonist, "but how did you know?"

"Well," said the woman, "you don't know where you are or where you're going. You have risen to where you are due to a large quantity of hot air. You made a promise, which you've no idea how to keep, and you expect people beneath you to solve your problems. The fact is, you are in exactly the same position you were in before we met. But now, somehow, it's my fault."

Trust ME...

There's only one way to be worthy of another person's trust, and that's to trust yourself. And the only way to trust yourself is to manage yourself. If *you* can count on you, then—and only then—can anyone else really count on you. Followers have an intuition about this. Trust me. (That is, if you think I've earned your trust.)

Leadership expert Tom Peters says that, ultimately, our whole economy runs on faith. He explains that shareholders invest because they have faith that the organization will prosper.[31]

I'd take that idea a step further: Our whole *lives* run on faith. I think all followers who invest in their leaders do so because they have faith in their leaders' abilities and judgment. Customers buy products in which they have faith. You don't get married to someone you don't trust—most of us wouldn't, anyway. You make plans for vacation assuming you're going to be around in three months to take that vacation. It's all about faith.

Now, this may seem like a left turn, but bear with me for a second. It's interesting to note that the strongest predictor of discretionary effort is autonomy; that is, the more people have a say in what they're doing, the more discretionary effort they'll give.[32]

And autonomy is all about faith. Autonomy requires leaders to have faith and trust in their followers. Continued autonomy requires followers to demonstrate they are trustworthy, thereby confirming the wisdom of the leader's faith.

In other words, the trustworthiness of your followers is related directly to the trust you, the leader, place in them. It's a mutual respect thing: you have faith in them and they have faith in you. And being a trustworthy leader requires trusting yourself.

See? It's all about faith.

...OR *Don't*

I've mentioned that followers can tell whether they can trust their leaders or not. How?

There are six telltale indications that a leader can't be trusted—six signs that the leader's vision of life is

inherently flawed and will inevitably lead to disaster
for the leader and, potentially, those who work for that
leader. Here they are:

1. The leader believes things will continue this way in perpetuity.
Denial of change is tantamount to denying the effects
of gravity before stepping off a 10-story building. The
results are universally disastrous. Stagnant leaders are
destined to have their world fly apart—and if you're a
follower, your world will fly apart, too. A leader who won't
recognize and adapt to change can't be trusted.

2. The leader believes the enemy comes from the outside.
The enemy is the competition. The enemy is that other
workgroup led by another manager. Pick an outside enemy,
and this leader will gladly point the finger. This sort of
belief is the result of fear-based thinking, and fear-based
people are dangerous people.

These leaders believe the source of their problems
and the answer to their difficulties lie somewhere else—
which means they're quick to assign blame. They'll blame
their supervisor, or the market conditions, or the supplier
or government regulations. Or you. They can't be trusted!

*3. The leader believes there are no long-term consequences
of today's decisions.* There are always consequences. These
consequences, positive or negative, will affect everyone
involved. You can't lie to make a sale today and think it's
not going to catch up with you. You can't squeeze your
vendors today and expect them to bail you out of a jam
tomorrow. If you think you can, you can't be trusted.

4. The leader is overly moody. Some leaders are guided by the weather—internal or external. They let external circumstances set their agenda, or they let their emotions rule the day(or both). If there's one thing everybody knows about the weather, it's that even meteorologists don't really know about the weather. It's unpredictable and unreliable. Just like this sort of leader.

5. The leader has poor relationships with loved ones. How can a leader be trusted if she can't get along with the people who have the most to gain or lose with her? If her loved ones can't trust her, then you can't either.

6. The leader is, in any area of his life, disrespectful of others. This is particularly pertinent when applied to how someone treats those who are most dependent on him or those who can't, by virtue of their position, talk back. In other words, how does the leader treat his kids or spouse or elderly parents, and how does he treat those who serve him in his everyday life—waiters, doormen, maids, et al? It has been said that you can tell a lot about a leader's true character by how they treat these folks. There is no easier or clearer way to see duplicity in a leader than to look at the presence or absence of respect in these types of relationships.

Remember, none of these factors of trustworthiness has anything to do with basic competence. They have nothing to do with what a leader does, and everything to do with what a leader is (although it's fair to point out the great leaders also *do* great things). To be a great leader, you must have competence and power. Competence can, in large part, be learned. Power must be awakened.

Which means that this power *must*, by definition, come from inside. The power of the leader is the power within.

This power within is not based on any of the usual contingencies. It's not based on promise of reward, coercion, threat, position or expertise. It's personal. It's at the heart and in the soul of every person on the planet. And it's real. It can be realized, embraced and experienced in profound ways over time.

The problem is, most of us don't even recognize that we have power within, and so the power lies dormant. We all have it, but not very many of us live it. And because we don't, most of us, in one or more of the ways above, to a greater or lesser degree, are untrustworthy leaders.

Common SENSE

We like common sense—and we like and respect people we believe have common sense. We like people who make good decisions based on what's in front of their faces. That's what common sense is: it's obvious, ordinary, general and practical. It's based on sensory experience. It's usually perceivable. It is the foundation of predictable, everyday behavior. As we say, "it's just common sense." On the flip side, it's difficult to respect someone who "doesn't have any common sense."

We like common sense because it offers a sense of security, consistency and commonality. Common sense is important in the competency of leadership. Common sense gives leaders their credibility.

Common sense says, "In general, the better you pay people, the harder they'll work and the more committed they'll be." Common sense says, "Keep pressure on your people and they'll stay more focused on what needs to get done." Common sense says, "Tell your followers what you need to have done, but don't be too open with them, because they won't really (and don't need to) understand the big picture."

But what we can see isn't everything there is. And sometimes the things that seem to be "just common sense" lead to conclusions that cause us pain. How many times have you heard stories of people who seemed to do everything right, but suffered devastating (yet predictable) consequences? How about the husband who worked 60 to 70 hours a week for the first ten years of his marriage, all the while believing that he was doing what every American husband and father does, only to find that he's lost the love of his wife—and, with their divorce, his time with their kids? Or, what about the wife who devotes so much time and attention to her kids that she neglects her husband? Or the executive whose processes and procedures have led to great business success, but who gets complacent, thinking that "doing what we've always been doing" will lead to success in perpetuity? Or the boss who's so focused on the bottom line that she barely notices her best people leaving the company? You've got to protect the bottom line; it's only common sense. But sometimes, in hindsight, common sense seems a little foolish.

The fact is, most of the time, we live our lives on automatic pilot, with little self-reflection; we function on common sense. But at some point, if we're thoughtful and honest, we come to realize that something isn't right. We're out of sync. We're at odds with ourselves. We're not living in accordance with what we know and believe.

The *Uncrisis*

There's a great song by the Talking Heads called, "Once in a Lifetime." It was made into a widely played music video back in the early '80s. Maybe you remember it. In part, it goes like this:

> *And you may find yourself living in a shotgun shack*
> *And you may find yourself in another part of the world*
> *And you may find yourself behind the wheel of a large automobile*
> *And you may find yourself in a beautiful house, with a beautiful wife*

And you may ask yourself: Well...how did I get here?
And you may ask yourself
How do I work this?
And you may ask yourself
Where is that large automobile?
And you may tell yourself
This is not my beautiful house!
And you may tell yourself
This is not my beautiful wife!

One of the song's choruses (it's a complicated song) consists of the singer saying, "Same as it ever was," over and over again. Put it all together, and the song seems to be about the disorienting effects of life in the modern world. Suddenly, the singer does not know where he is. Nothing makes sense. Everything seems foreign—possessions, relationships, his position in life, the way he relates to the world—and yet, everything is the same as it ever was. He's out of sorts, over his head; another of the other recurring images in the song involves drowning.

He's been living a life based on common sense—and nothing makes sense anymore.

"Once in a Lifetime" is a portrait of a man in crisis. But where's the crisis—which we might define as a powerful emotional event or a point of radical change? Everything looks okay. It's the same as it ever was. There's no event. There's no point. Whatever's happening that's so unsettling must come from within.

Call it "the Uncrisis." The Uncrisis may come about
suddenly. But more often than not, it happens gradually.
It creeps up on you. And it really is a connection to
something deep and basic about your life—something
that really is the same as it ever was. It's a realization that
living a life based on common sense is somehow terribly
unsatisfying—because *life is not based on common sense.*

A Common-SENSE
Fable

Once upon a time, there lived a fifteen-year-old girl in a
small Midwestern town. The girl was smart, pretty and
ambitious, according to the social conventions of the
time in which she grew up. She attended school and
church and helped with chores around the house, and
was well liked and admired by her friends.

One day, this girl met a boy. Strike that: this boy was
a man. He was nineteen, and he was every bit her match:
handsome, intelligent, ambitious, filled with a love of life
and a hunger to make his way in the world. The girl was
smitten, and the young man was besotted. This was no
schoolgirl crush, no romantic fling: this was love.

And, as so often happens when two people are in love (or even in a crush or a fling or less), the girl and the young man consummated their relationship. And, a little over a month later, the girl discovered that the consummation had had an unintended, but completely predictable, consequence.

Our young lovers were frightened, but determined. They would get married. They would make their way in the world together. They would have this child and raise this child and love this child, and it would be difficult for them, but what is difficulty in the face of true love?

The girl's parents had a different idea.

Her life was ruined. She was too young to have a child, and far too young to be married—especially to someone so much older and more experienced than she. They didn't know anything about this young man, other than his quite obvious lack of virtue and respect for their daughter. It simply did not make sense to allow this to happen. It would be far better for everyone for the girl to slip away quietly, give up her baby, come back to resume her schooling, put herself back on a path to having a normal life. This was a setback, but it wasn't too late.

The young man's parents agreed. He was too young to take a wife and have the responsibility of a family. He was a brilliant young man. He didn't need a child holding him back. The girl herself was a child. A child with a child, and the ruination of a promising young man's life. Common sense said this would be a terrible, terrible mistake.

Can you deny it, dear Reader? Can you imagine your reaction if the girl were your own beautiful daughter? If the young man were your own handsome son? Would it not be best for everyone to break this couple apart and allow them to resume the lives they had planned?

As it turns out, it wouldn't have been best for me—or, for that matter, many others—because the girl was my grandmother. And the young man was my grandfather. And the child was my father. My dad: an energetic, loving, committed husband and father dedicated not only to his family, but also to thousands of others by way of his 50 years of pastoral care.

Life doesn't obey the rules of common sense. That's why relying on common sense throughout our lives usually leads us to a place where everything is the same as it ever was, but nothing seems right.

Anguish

So, what is it? We go along, living our lives, trying to do right by our families and friends and coworkers and employees. We live by common sense, because—well, that's just what we do, isn't it? When we're faced with decisions, we weigh the consequences we can foresee and do what we think is best.

And yet, we can't possibly know what's best in the long run. If my grandparents had done what their families thought best—what, undeniably, made sense—I wouldn't be here today. How can we know?

We can't. And so we wake up one day, and everything is the same, only different. It's like the old Stephen Wright joke: "One morning, I got up and discovered that someone had replaced everything in my apartment with an exact replica."

Where does this feeling come from? Why do we all feel it? And what in the world does it have to do with leadership?

This unsettledness is *anguish*—and it is *not* a feeling. Feelings are far more situational: a coworker insults you, so you feel hurt or angry. But you go home and your spouse tells you how wonderful you are, and you laugh at a comedian you see on TV, and, before you know it, you feel better. Feelings are temporary.

Anguish isn't. Anguish is a sort of background. It's the belief that something is wrong. It's always there, in spite of what you may be feeling from moment to moment. In fact, its omnipresence is what makes anguish so devastating. I've seen people laughing and having a good time one moment, yet reporting that even in their "good time", something just doesn't seem right. It's a background experience that dampens even the best of times.

Or, according to renowned author Huston Smith, "There is within us—in even the blithest, most lighthearted among us—a fundamental *dis-ease*. It acts like an unquenchable fire that renders the vast majority of us incapable in this life of ever coming to full peace. This desire lies in the marrow of our bones and deep in the regions of our soul. All great literature, poetry, art, philosophy, psychology and religion try to name and analyze this longing. We are seldom in direct touch with it, and indeed the modern world seems set on preventing us from getting in touch with it by covering it with an unending phantasmagoria of entertainment, obsessions and distractions of every sort. But the longing is there, built into us like a jack-in-the-box that presses for release... whether we realize it or not, simply to be human is to long for release from the mundane existence with its confining walls of finitude and mortality." [33]

And we all experience it. Anguish is not clinical depression. In fact, I've come to believe that much of what people complain about as depression or anxiety is actually neither. It's anguish. I believe that we have created a mind-altering, antidepressant society in a vain attempt to escape the misery of this ubiquitous anguish.

Anguish is the result of living a life based on common sense. *Because life doesn't really follow the rules of common sense.* What seems sensible in the short term often leads to disaster. What seems like a disaster now can turn into a positive and beautiful thing in the long run.

The good news is, if you are aware of the experience of anguish, it can lead to an awakening. Actually, every aspect of life is based on an underlying, unseen reality that we seldom consider. It's not really common sense, but *uncommon sense*—and it's the key to being able to effectively manage yourself, and thus to being a great leader. Like common sense, uncommon sense is sane, reasonable, even observable, although seldom in a material way. But it's often forgotten or ignored. That's what's so uncommon about it.

INTERMISSION:
ALL CHANGE

....

Anguish & CHANGE

Recognizing anguish is no small thing. When you recognize your experience of anguish, you can begin to initiate change.

Maybe you're not yet ready to take action. Maybe you're still thinking about where your life is headed and what you should be doing that you're not. Maybe you're not thinking about it consciously at all yet. That's okay. Remember what I said at the start of this book: you don't have to *do* anything.

But now we've arrived at a place where we're ready to make a leap: a leap from talking about living a life based on common sense to a life based on uncommon sense. We're going to talk about change. So, we'd best begin by talking about the formal process of change.

We often think of change as an event: we're going to change starting…*now*. We're going to lose weight. We're going to stop smoking. We're going to be better parents. There's going to be a dividing line between right now, when we change, and everything that came before.

Actually, change is not an event, but a nonlinear process that appears to have certain predictable stages.[34] These stages do have a progressive order, and they're always experienced in this order; that is, you can't skip a stage. But it's never a straight line from here to there. The process consists of starts and stops, progression and regression, and it varies in length. In other words, you can get stuck along the way.

So, let's talk a little bit about change—specifically with regard to anguish. In fact, let's take half a step back and talk about what happens *before* you recognize anguish, which is actually the first stage of the formalized process of change: the *pre-contemplative state.*[35]

The person in pre-contemplation doesn't acknowledge the need to change. Others around you may know you need to change, but you're not thinking about it at all. Pre-contemplation is a state void of self-reflection. In pre-contemplation, you simply react to what's going on around you. You're reflexive, and not reflective.

You're also not alone: at any given time, 40 percent of any group is in pre-contemplation. And that may be a conservative figure these days, especially in business, where the demands of the Information Age force so many of us to spend our time reacting instead of reflecting. After all, engaging the hearts and minds of your employees can take years—and you need results right now. But if you don't start to break out of pre-contemplation, you'll have missed your window of opportunity completely. Remember: engaged, trusting employees willing to give more discretionary effort are your market advantage.

Or, think about the parents of teens who seem to believe that their job is to restrict and protect their children rather than relate to them and prepare them to live in the world. I recently heard a parent say, "I wish I'd spent less time preparing the road for my children and had spent more time preparing my children for the road." She apparently had been pre-contemplative of the change she would have made in raising her kids.

With this sort of reflection, you begin to recognize the need for change. By looking back at the past and projecting forward into the future, you can get a sense of where your life is going and what you need to do to make it better. You step away from the hustle and bustle of your everyday activity, into thoughts and feelings about where your current path is leading. This is where the pre-contemplation ends and the *contemplation stage* begins.

In any group, at any given time, 40 percent are in contemplation.[36] This stage, which often lasts for six months, involves much introspection and consideration of what you could do differently in order to be more in sync, better integrated and in less anguish (even if you don't really recognize anguish as anguish). You're increasingly thoughtful about your current condition and how making a change would affect your life. You observe your life from the outside, with that part of you—a part of all of us—that simply watches, takes in what's going on, quietly, reflectively and intuitively. It is here, in this observing part of ourselves, that we begin to find wisdom and awaken to the power within.

The next stage in the process of change is *preparation*.

This stage usually lasts no longer than a month or two and involves that process of "lining things out" so that lasting change is more likely. At any given time, only 20 percent of any group is in preparation for change.[37]

Preparation is exactly what it says: positioning for the act of change. You look back at how things have been and then look forward to how things would be if you could be free of the problems that are troubling you. As you get deeper into preparation, you increasingly believe that you *can* change.

Finally, you make a commitment to act on that belief. You decide you *will* stop smoking, and you set a date for abstinence, tell your friends you're going to stop, and buy lots of gum. You *will* shore up your relationships with your loved ones—so you begin to cut your excessive work hours, drop out of one of your two golf leagues, and make a date night with your spouse. This is preparation.

Now, here's an interesting statistic: One in five persons (20 percent of any group) is ready for change[38]...and 20 percent of any group is considered the critical mass needed to actually effect change. What this means is that engaging just the people who are ready for change can revolutionize an organization. Imagine if 50 or 60 percent could be engaged; what if even 40 percent of the organization could be brought along? But change is a process, not an event. You have to respect the change process as an individual. And organizations have to respect the individual change process, as well.

The fourth phase of the change process is *action.*[39] These are people already in the act of change and no longer in the process of change. In the action phase, you actually do what you've agonized over and thought about and planned and prepared to do.

That's how change happens. But just going through the change process doesn't get you past the trap of common sense. Every great leader, expressly or intuitively, understands that life is not based on common sense. So, if you're going to make the effort to change, I recommend you embark upon a plan of change that can actually make a difference in your life, and in the lives of the people you lead, by learning the Six Universal Principles of Uncommon Sense.

The 6 UNIVERSAL PRINCIPLES of *Uncommon Sense*

First: you'll find no earth-shattering revelations here. As I have said, I have no magic bullet. Chances are, you've been presented with most or all of the principles that follow at one time or another in your life. Several of these principles are common enough that you might even think of them as clichés.

Frankly, that's part of the problem. When a universal principle strikes you as a cliché, it loses its power. So, I'm going to remind you once again to read with an open mind. Dig a little deeper. While none of these principles will be a surprise—because they're all universally observed and experienced, they are, as our Founding Fathers said, self evident—I think you'll find them to be surprisingly powerful when you consider them carefully.

These universal principles are a reality behind the reality of our everyday life. They are consistent, predictable and inevitable. Every one of these Principles of Uncommon Sense is derived from how life actually works—and, even if you're familiar with the basic ideas, I doubt you have ever examined them in the depth you're going to in the pages that follow.

The Principles of Uncommon Sense reflect how life actually works. That's a pretty bold statement. Anyone want to challenge me on that?

I thought you might. I know this because I've had the opportunity to share the most intimate thoughts and feelings of thousands of people over the past 25 years. I have witnessed firsthand how these six consistent Principles of Uncommon Sense make the difference in how people experience or lead their lives. I've also seen that people routinely ignore them at their own peril. Every patient I've ever seen has been suffering as a result of ignoring one of these principles and denying its wisdom in guiding his or her actions.

This is not a new method of leading life or leading others; there have always been people living and leading this way, many of whom have come by these principles intuitively, without conscious thought or effort. These principles are not a "to-do" list. These are not steps to better living or better leadership. They are simply things to consider, to ponder, to contemplate. They may cause you to be less reflexive and more reflective. As a consequence, your experience of life may be different, better.

And, if you're leading a better life, you become a better leader.

Remember, it's not what you *do,* but rather what you *are* that makes a difference. When we have a problem or a situation we want to change, our culture tends to push us toward *changing our life experience,* when, in reality, we need a *change in our experience of life.* Perhaps you really don't have to do anything. You just have to change how you experience things.

If you truly acknowledge and consider them, these six principles will transform you and your experience of life—every aspect of your experience. The research suggests that these uncommon sense principles ultimately lead to health and happiness. My experience suggests that, as well. I'm betting your experience will agree.

THE FIRST
UNIVERSAL PRINCIPLE
OF UNCOMMON SENSE

....

THE PRINCIPLE OF

THE HARVEST:

AS YOU *sow*,

SO SHALL YOU *reap*

....

UP from the *Muck*

He was a poor Scottish farmer named Fleming. He worked the hard land, barely scraping by year after year, making just enough to support his family.

One day, Fleming was out in his field when he heard a cry for help coming from a nearby bog. He dropped his tools and ran. There, mired to his waist in black muck, was a terrified boy screaming and struggling to free himself. The lad's struggles were causing him to sink lower into the goo. But Farmer Fleming calmed him and slowly pulled him out of the bog. Fleming saved the boy from what could have been a slow and terrifying death.

The next day, a fancy carriage pulled up to Fleming's simple homestead. An elegantly dressed nobleman stepped out and introduced himself as the father of the boy Farmer Fleming had saved. "I want to repay you," said the nobleman. "You saved my son's life."

"No, I can't accept payment for what I did," the farmer replied, waving off the offer.

At that moment, the farmer's own son came to the door of the family hovel. "Is this your son?" the nobleman asked.

"Yes," the farmer replied proudly. "He's a bright boy, as well."

"I'll make you a deal, then," said the nobleman. "Let me provide the boy with the level of education my own son will enjoy. If the lad is anything like his father, he'll no doubt grow to be a man we will both be proud of."

And that he did. Farmer Fleming's son attended the very best schools in the British Isles. In time, the younger Fleming was graduated from St. Mary's Hospital Medical School in London. Perhaps you've heard of him: Sir Alexander Fleming went on to become known throughout the world as the discoverer of penicillin.

Ironically, years later, that same nobleman's son who was saved from the bog was stricken with pneumonia. It was penicillin that saved the life of the nobleman's son.

Have I neglected to mention that the nobleman's name was Lord Randolph Churchill? And that the boy who was pulled from the muck—whose life was saved again, many years later, by penicillin—was Winston Churchill?

Not-so-instant
Karma

We're all moved and mystified by stories like the one about Alexander Fleming and Winston Churchill. You may not specifically identify this as a story about the

Principle of the Harvest[40]—that is, that we reap what we sow, or we get what we give—but you know, at some level, that this sort of occurrence is evidence of this, the most familiar of the six principles. Often referred to as *karma*, the Principle of the Harvest is a cornerstone of every major faith tradition in the world. It's so readily apparent and acknowledged that the Beatles not only sang about it, but also made it the capstone statement of their entire songbook: "And in the end, the love you take is equal to the love you make." Can Jesus, Mohammed, the Buddha, King Solomon, John, Paul, George *and* Ringo be wrong?

We readily accept this principle when it comes to the things we desire in life. We believe that if we work diligently, our hard work will pay off. We know that the more education we get, the more likely we'll get to do what we want to do in life and the greater our income over our lifetime (if that's what we're looking to get). We know that regular exercise begets better health, more energy and a sense of well-being. We know that if we save and invest for retirement, we'll be more financially secure in our later years. The Protestant work ethic… delayed gratification…we grew up with these ideas, and we can confirm that they're true. They may not play out as common sense—in fact, it would seem to make more sense to take this afternoon off, because you have only one life and you might as well enjoy it right now. You don't know what's going to happen in the future. Why worry about it?

Because, perhaps more than any of the other Universal Principles of Uncommon Sense, you have actually experienced the Principle of the Harvest. You saved your money for months and, sure enough, you had enough to buy a bicycle. You studied hard and put off partying and did get that degree. You put up with a crummy, oppressive boss for three years, just so you could get the experience you needed to take the next step in your job. You sacrificed *now* to get something better *later.*

So, it's always a wonder to me that, with this degree of universal familiarity and acceptance, so many people live as if this principle doesn't apply to them. We tend to accept the Principle of the Harvest regarding the things we want, but not when it applies to the things we'd rather avoid. I'm sure the thinking goes something like this: "Oh, I know it's true, but somehow I'll be able to stop what I'm doing before it catches up with me." Or, "My grandfather drank six beers and smoked a pack of cigarettes every day, starting when he was 15, and he lived to be 93." As if, just like dear old Grandpa, you'll be the exception and not the rule.

SAME as You *Sow,* MORE Than You *Sow,* *Later* Than You *Sow*

In my clinical experience, violation of The Principle of the Harvest is more often the cause of people's emotional and relational pain than any other single thing. It's not that they don't know the principle; usually, they know it very well. It's one of those things that, if you reflect on it, you know is true. Even so, we seem to forget it or ignore it when it's inconvenient. We certainly don't respect it when it gets in the way of immediate gratification.

To put it another way, when it comes to the Principle of the Harvest, we actually lie to ourselves. We're not honest about the potentially devastating consequences of our self-destructive behavior.

And yet, we're very aware of the same principle when it comes to things we consciously want. We apply the principle selectively. The very same people who employ the Principle of the Harvest in their education and their business and their retirement accounts suddenly lapse into ignorance when it comes to their marriage, relating to their kids and taking care of their health. Curious, isn't it?

To this point, my explanation of the Principle of the Harvest has been a little cursory. Actually, the Principle of the Harvest says that *you reap what you sow: the same as you sow, more than you sow, later than you sow.*[41] Consider this carefully: it's what you sow, more than you sow, but later than you sow. It takes a full season to harvest your plantings.

Of course, it's called the Principle of the Harvest because it's best exemplified in farming. All farmers live by this natural law. They would never plant corn and expect to harvest soybeans: you reap the same as you sow. That's just the way it is. They know with a high degree of likelihood that they will get much more back at harvest than they planted: you reap more than you sow. They are also patient, realizing that there is a season to plant, a season for growing, and a season of harvest: you reap later than you sow.

These are such basic and assumed principles in farming that it's ludicrous to consider that it could be done any other way. There's no sense—uncommon or otherwise—in planting corn and expecting to harvest beans. Or in harvesting one kernel of corn for every kernel you plant. And any farmer who takes his combine to the fields in June will find nothing to harvest. These notions seem ridiculous.

Bankers understand this principle when it comes to investing. Over time, a smart investment yields a strong return. Health care professionals are all too aware of the consequences of living in violation of the Principle of the

Harvest. In fact, it is estimated that, on any given day, 50 percent of this country's hospital beds are occupied by patients who have not been compliant with treatment recommendations. Even physicists have their own kind of Principle of the Harvest that says that for every action there is an equal and opposite reaction.

We all know it's true. So, why do we run our personal lives as if it's not?

Why BAD Things Happen to *Smart* PEOPLE

My business partner Steve smoked for many years. Steve wasn't what you'd consider a heavy smoker; he smoked, maybe, a pack a day. As you may recall, Steve was a physician, so he had no excuses: he knew the consequences of smoking all too well. He was also a psychiatrist and, therefore, knew that people have a tendency to deny that bad things can happen to them, and he understood the psychology and physiology of addiction. Add to this the fact that Steve's father had died of heart disease, so he knew he had an increased, genetically based propensity to coronary conditions. He had no good reason to continue smoking, and lots of good reasons to quit; yet, he continued to smoke.

On April 1, 1997—I remember the date because I thought he was playing an April Fool's joke on me— Steve came to my office and told me he had been having chest pain: several episodes of chest pain over the previous couple of weeks. He assured me, I suppose both as a friend and a responsible business partner, that he'd have it checked out.

Several angioplasties later, after Steve's arteries persisted in closing even over the stents that had been inserted to keep them open, the decision was made to do a quadruple coronary bypass. Three months later, on July first, at age 44, this eminently sensible man and brilliant healer underwent bypass surgery.

After the operation, I went to see Steve in coronary intensive care. As he lay in his hospital bed with tubes running in and out all over his body, I said, "Bet you don't want a cigarette now, do you?"

I'll never forget what he said. "You know, Greg," said Steve, the regret almost palpable in his voice, "I always thought I'd quit before this happened."

Amazing. This man whom I loved as a friend and admired as the best psychiatrist I'd ever worked with— this man who clearly understood the use of denial and rationalization as a defense mechanism to keep from having to confront conflict and dissonance—was himself a victim of self-deception. It was never more clear to me that the Principle of the Harvest, this simple law that everyone knows, but few of us really live by, has nothing to do with common sense and everything to do with uncommon sense.

The Four
Lies

The Principle of the Harvest, as familiar as it is, remains uncommon sense because, at least in some area of our lives, we act as if it doesn't exist. There are four self-deceptions or myths—or, if you want to cut the sugar coating, out-and-out lies—we tell ourselves that cause us to ignore this principle. These lies are subtle. No one would dare to speak them aloud; yet, if we're honest, as Steve was following his bypass surgery, we have to admit we've been seduced by them.

The First Lie: "I'll apply the principle selectively: I'll live by it, get what I want in some areas of my life, and I'll ignore it in all the other areas." This is what happens when people are tremendously successful in business or some other area of life, but have disastrous personal lives. They live by the principle in their work, then forget it when they go home in the evening. Another example: people who exercise diligently, eat right, perhaps have minor cosmetic surgery to keep themselves looking young and fit, but then, consistent with their effort to look good, overexpose themselves to the sun or tanning lights. They recognize the Principle of the Harvest as it applies to their appearance, but ignore it when considering the risk of skin cancer.

Another way this lie plays out is the tragedy of unintended consequences: you intend to pay attention to the Principle of the Harvest, but through subtle self-deception or lack of perspective, you create collateral damage. For example, a man I knew worked diligently for 60 or 70 hours a week while his kids were growing up. Aaron truly loved his wife and kids for all he was worth, and convinced himself and his wife that he had to continue his insane work schedule so they could provide a better life for their kids. You know the rest of the story: in his narrow view of what his kids needed, Aaron lost sight of their larger need to have him present in their lives.

This is duplicity, this idea that you can have it all— that you can work 70 hours a week to build your business and still be a good father. Duplicity brings unintended consequences. The truth is: You can't do it all, and you can't have it all. To believe otherwise is to lie to yourself.

The Second Lie: "It won't happen to me." This is blatant, flat-out denial. In my clinical practice, I see the results of denial all the time. It's a sort of "forgetting" what you know. But there's usually still a subtle awareness of the inevitability of a harvest. Most people who deny the Principle of the Harvest will actually admit to the denial with mild confrontation.

The Third Lie: "I'll be able to anticipate the consequences and head off the disaster." This is the lie my buddy Steve bought into; in my experience, it's the most common path to disaster, especially for sophisticated, educated people who can't deny the Principle of the Harvest, but still don't live by it. The very fact that they are bright and educated may cause them to have a sort of arrogance about being able to somehow outsmart the natural order. It's a lie, of course, most likely born of hubris.

The Fourth Lie: "The principle doesn't apply to me." This is certainly a defiant declaration. It's different from "it won't happen to me" in that the defiance is not denial of the principle, but rather opposition to the natural order, as if you're somehow above it. This is hubris of the highest order. I most often see this lie in people who are emotionally immature. It's an adolescent style of bravado, but it can be observed in people of all ages.

You'll note that none of these lies is based on an inability to understand the Principle of the Harvest or to witness the evidence of its presence. The principle is self-evident for anyone who pauses to reflect even momentarily. It is sensible both in that it can be witnessed with the senses and that it makes logical sense. But it remains uncommon for someone to live its reality in a comprehensive way.

You are *Your Own* WORST ENEMY

There's another side to the Principle of the Harvest. While it's true that what you do today will ultimately yield what happens tomorrow, it's also true that where you find yourself today is the result of what you did yesterday. That is, whatever you are experiencing now, your current situation is likely to be the consequence, to a greater or lesser degree, of the seed you've sown. If you're at a place in your life that you don't like, it's your own doing. Look at your circumstance, consider what it is you're reaping, and know that it's likely the result of the seed you've sown—plus that all-important "growing season."

If you've been blessed with a great deal of prosperity, look to see what you've done that would explain your success. If you're fortunate enough to be deeply loved by people in your life, consider how you've related to them to have gained such affection. Likewise, if you've had the misfortune of being betrayed by someone you love, look to see if you've betrayed another at sometime in the past.

The importance of giving this manifestation of the Principle of the Harvest its due is that it shortstops a lot of time and energy you might otherwise waste in pride.

Some people boast of their accomplishments and success as if they were personal. To some degree, they *are* personal. But, to a larger degree, they're the consequence of having sown the proper seed and let it grow. Your success is attributable less to something you did than to your having heeded the Principle of the Harvest, consciously or not.

On the other hand, some people pine away for days, weeks, months, even years about the injustices they've had to endure. We've all known people who just never seem to be able to get past the terrible wrongs done to them. And indeed, in a few—a precious few—situations, terrible injustices do occur. But the vast majority of the time, the injustices are simply the consequences of not paying attention to the Principle of the Harvest. And the people stuck in the injustices they think have been done to them are those who not only didn't attend to this universal principle, but also continue to ignore it.

We don't often think about it this way, but self-pity— this idea that somehow you are not going to experience the consequences of the same natural law we all live by—is based in pride. It could be the result of denial, but it's more likely the result of arrogance and self-aggrandizement. In any event, self-pity is worthless in the economy of uncommon sense.

REVENGE vs. *Peace*

If you don't acknowledge it, the Principle of the Harvest can drain you of energy; if you do acknowledge it, it energizes you. If you adhere to this principle and you appreciate that it applies to all of us, then you have no reason, ever, for resentment—or, more importantly, for revenge. In the politics of the world, business or personal, taking names and getting even may seem like the prudent thing to do. But it's a colossal waste of energy when living in the uncommon-sense awareness of the Principle of the Harvest. And if the principle holds true, taking revenge now will come back to hurt you later.

No doubt, there are examples of leaders who experienced injustices and were able, with swift adeptness, to exact vengeance on a competitor or even cohort who "got in the way." Maybe you know some stories like this. And it may appear, on the surface and in the short run, that these leaders have won. It may even, in some cases, appear as if the bad guys got their comeuppance and the vengeful leader used her power for good.

But did she really? Time and again, I've encountered titans of industry who have lived their business lives ruthlessly and succeeded magnificently—only to spend their later years begging for a single meaningful relationship with a loved one. Did they really think they could plant the

seeds of selfishness and pettiness in their work relationships and not have it affect their personal lives? Duplicity
is bondage. To leave your heart at home when you go to
work is disastrous; what happens is that your heart
disappears altogether. There's no such thing as "just
business." "Just business" may be common sense, but it's
not uncommon sense.

If you really understand the Principle of the Harvest,
you'll realize that you never have to exact revenge against
a person who's wronged you. The principle ensures that
if you are done wrong by another, that person will experience
the consequences of his behavior without your having to
do a thing. There are natural consequences, and you're
not in charge of them.

Of course, letting the Principle of the Harvest take
its course requires self-control and patience. It requires
a good deal of faith that the principle is real and works
in everyone's life: yours, mine, your friends' and your
enemies'. But I'm here to tell you that it doesn't require
blind faith. My 60,000 hours of experience addressing
people's distress has shown me that the Principle of the
Harvest holds true over and over again. In some situations,
it seems that people who have wronged you will defeat
themselves, almost as if they knew they had it coming; in
other cases, the unseen consequences of the lies and
self-deception catch up with them; and sometimes it
seems their negative harvest is inexplicable, perhaps the
result of a mystical ordering of the universe. Seldom do

the consequences occur right away (remember, *later than you sow*), and almost never is the person injured by the original injustice, the one responsible for the ultimate karmic payback. In fact, in my experience, if you move on and stop holding onto the need for revenge, by the time the Principle of the Harvest catches up with your tormenter, you'll actually feel sadness, even pity, for him.

It's a relief to know that you don't have to be responsible for cosmic justice. To embrace the Principle of the Harvest and forgive others for what they've done, knowing that it's not your place to mete out the consequences for their actions, leads to contentment, satisfaction, happiness and serenity. Living with and by this uncommon sense brings peace.

Grow UP*!*

We love dramatic justice. We love it when bad things happen to bad people and the good guys win in the end. That's why, so often in our lives, the Principle of the Harvest comes up with regard to negative consequences. But this principle should be, and actually is, more about celebration than tragedy. You can just as easily benefit from recognizing the Principle of the Harvest as you can suffer by ignoring it. But gaining these benefits requires personal maturity.

What is personal maturity? It's obviously not age;
we all know people of advanced age who are not mature.
It's not position; some of the most powerful people in the
world most certainly act immaturely. It's not seriousness of
demeanor; maturity is not dourness, and people who are
the most mature actually have the most raucous adventures
of life. It has nothing to do with success in business.
So, what is it? How can you recognize maturity in yourself
or someone else?

Very simply, personal maturity is the ability to step
outside yourself, away from your own personal wishes,
and take a broader view of the world. The greater your
personal maturity, the greater your vision and the
broader your perspective—the sort of broad perspective
required to delay immediate gratification in favor of a
delayed, but more bountiful harvest.

Developing personal maturity requires personal
reflection, which grows from the practice of suspending
or "witnessing" yourself. Witnessing is something we've
all done, but have seldom considered—and have probably
even been discouraged from doing. It is a process whereby
we observe our lives as a whole *and* as we're living them
day by day. We reflect not only on what we're doing and
saying, but also what we're thinking and feeling.

Perhaps an illustration will help. Witnessing is like
flying at ground level, but with the perspective of being
at ten thousand feet in the air. If you flew at ground level
with only ground-level perspective, you'd be so occupied

with the next obstacle that it would be quite easy to lose sight of where you were in relation to your destination. But flying at ground level with a ten-thousand-foot perspective greatly improves your ability to see how the same upcoming obstacle could be best negotiated in relation to reaching your destination. In other words, witnessing is like the Global Positioning System. If you have the GPS in your car, it provides perspective and keeps the destination in sight. Oh, if only we could program our desired destination in life and then have a GPS know where to turn and what bridges were out and could help us avoid dead ends. Well—that's what personal maturity does. It provides you with a personal GPS.

Witnessing is somewhat dispassionate and not judgmental. So, rather than saying to yourself during a moment of reflection, "That's wrong," or, "You shouldn't have done that," or, "You shouldn't feel that way," or, "That's a crazy way of thinking," you think, "Hmm, now…that's interesting." You see, your immediate judgments about events in your life, be they confrontations with a coworker or hurt feelings about something your wife said or thoughts about what you ate for dinner, are part of the reason that you deceive yourself with the lies and myths. Being curious, but nonjudgmental of your experience, brings less shame and fosters more honest reflection.

Now, of course, you can't stop with curiosity; rather, the next aspect of witnessing is to consider whether what you're doing, saying, feeling or thinking is going to bring the harvest you desire. If it's not, you have the opportunity to change what you're doing.

So, in terms of leading a life, it makes sense to encourage witnessing. If you're just "paying attention", you end up sleepwalking through life. Awakening to the power within requires seeing through or past those things that common sense would have you attend to so you can benefit from uncommon sense.

The *First* PRINCIPLE at Work in Your *Organization*

We spent a little time discussing the idea of discretionary effort in the workplace. Discretionary effort is actually an example of the Principle of the Harvest at work on an organizational level. You get back effort from your employees based on how you treat them; they are willing to give more effort now for a larger reward at a later time. As the percentage of discretionary effort given increases, so do employee satisfaction and retention. And, of course, we know that employee retention is the most significant contributing factor to customer satisfaction. So, according to the Principle of the Harvest, treating employees in a way that encourages discretionary effort is great for the organization in the long run.

Unfortunately, organizations tend to ignore the Principle of the Harvest the same way individuals do. Many organizations deceive themselves about how they're dealing with employees. They think the Principle of the Harvest doesn't apply to them or that they'll somehow be able to head off the consequences. Research shows that more than 87 percent of businesses that have been informed of this powerful principle fail to embrace it.[42]

This is almost tragic. Because research also shows that companies that really do put their people first, the roughly 12 percent of organizations that really do embrace their people as their strategy, are the companies that, over time, regardless of industry and market conditions, outperform the competition.[43] It's the Principle of the Harvest at work.

I know of a small organization with a reputation for treating its employees in a very "businesslike" fashion—which is code, I think, for "what can you do for me?" At least, that's how the employees feel. Many employees question whether they're treated fairly. As you can imagine, employee turnover is high and customer satisfaction is low. Whatever the company is saving by managing the organization in this way, it's losing in rehiring costs, poor employee retention and customer alienation. Is it any wonder that the company also discovered that one of its administrators had been embezzling?

Of course, the embezzling may have happened anyway, but how much did that employee's sense that she wasn't being treated fairly play in to her decision to take what wasn't hers? We know that, psychologically, people often take what they want because they are not getting what they need. If we believe the research, what she may have wanted was simply for someone at work to care about her.

The fact is, just as individual maturity is required to embrace the Principle of the Harvest in your personal life, so a level of organizational maturity is required to allow the principle to work to an organization's advantage. An organization also has to "witness" the seed it's planting and imagine what harvest is likely to result. It's the antithesis of short-term focus, which is so often the result of looking at the numbers alone.

Likewise, we can see the importance of the Principle of the Harvest in the most common organization in this country: the family. Parents who plant the seeds of compassion, sensitivity, loyalty, togetherness, love and empathy are much more likely to have a healthier, more functional family system.

Ultimately, though, it all comes back to individuals— which means it comes back to *you*. All organizations, whether families or businesses, are made up of individuals. No family can be functional and no business can be healthy unless there are healthy, mature individuals in the organization who understand the uncommon sense of the Principle of the Harvest.

A COUPLE *of Hints*

Lest you think that I'd leave you to your own devices
to figure out what seed you're sowing, let me give you a
couple of general ideas that can help you awaken to the
power of the Principle of the Harvest.

First, consider the research done in the last ten years
by Dr. Mihaly Csikszentmihalyi on what brings people
the greatest sense of well-being in life. Csikszentmihalyi
is an academic psychologist interested in the optimal
human experiences: well-being, satisfaction and performance.
He reflects on the pursuits of "pleasure" and "enjoyment",
and his findings are interesting: people who seek pleasure
have less of a sense of well-being and satisfaction than
people whose actions lead to enjoyment.[44] Csikszentmihalyi
defines pleasure as the good feeling you get when you
satisfy basic physical needs. It's the result of instant
gratification and low effort. Enjoyment, on the other
hand, is related to pushing yourself beyond mere comfort
to new levels of personal growth and life satisfaction.
Enjoyment is the consequence of high effort and delayed
gratification.

So, wolfing down your favorite fast food—in my case,
French fries—provides instant gratification with low
effort, comfort with little cost involved (at least in the
short run—the Principle of the Harvest is going to catch

up with your bad eating habits over time). On the other hand, stopping by the market to pick up vegetables for a salad and then going home and making the salad is delaying gratification and working harder to be gratified, while also being healthier for me. Or consider the ease of taking a nap versus the effort of taking a walk. Or, what about the low effort of watching television as opposed to the greater effort of reading a good book?

In general, the rule is that sowing the seeds related to high effort and delayed gratification yields a harvest of greater overall enjoyment in life. And, of course, low effort and immediate gratification yield a life-experience harvest of poorer quality. Makes sense, doesn't it? Well... judging by the number of us who choose easy, immediate satisfaction, it makes "uncommon sense."

If you think about it, the Principle of the Harvest is saying three things. First, you *will* have a harvest, so consider carefully what you want to happen in your life. In fact, you may think of your life as a continual harvest; you're always sowing and you're always reaping something. Second, what your life eventually becomes is related directly to what you are doing today and every day. In other words, there is an order, a cause and effect, to your life. What you do today matters for today and for tomorrow. And third, there is a "season" during which the seed becomes the harvest. It is the ability to understand this Principle of the Harvest that allows us to see through our everyday experience to the reality that lies beyond.

It's quite simple, really. If you remember back to the first part of this book, I told you that you didn't have to *do* anything. And you don't have to *do* anything for the Principle of the Harvest to work. It already works; it simply *is*. The question is, what will your harvest be? Because you really don't have to do anything. But what you do makes all the difference in your life.

The *First* Principle
SUMMARIZED

- The Principle of the Harvest says that *you reap what you sow: the same as you sow, more than you sow, later than you sow.*

- There are Four Lies we tell ourselves that cause us to ignore this principle:

I'll apply the principle selectively: I'll live by it, get what I want in some areas of my life, and I'll ignore it in all the other areas."

"It won't happen to me."

"I'll be able to anticipate the consequences and head off the disaster."

A defiant declaration: "The principle doesn't apply to me."

- Whatever you are experiencing now, your current situation is likely to be the consequence, to a greater or lesser degree, of the seed you've sown.

- If you adhere to this principle and you appreciate that it applies to all of us, then you have no reason, ever, for resentment—or, more importantly, for revenge.

- Personal maturity is the ability to step outside yourself, away from your own personal wishes, and take a broader view of the world. The greater your personal maturity, the greater your vision and the broader your perspective.

- The Principle of the Harvest at work on an organizational level: You get back effort from your employees based on how you treat them; they are willing to give more effort now for a larger reward at a later time. As the percentage of discretionary effort given increases, so do employee satisfaction and retention. And, of course, we know that employee retention is the most significant contributing factor to customer satisfaction.

THE SECOND
UNIVERSAL PRINCIPLE
OF UNCOMMON SENSE

THE PRINCIPLE OF THE

COMMON DENOMINATOR:

IT'S *all*

ABOUT *you*

Therapy *Stories*

Charles, a 38-year-old patient, was having marital problems. He and his wife, Sherry, had been married for 15 years. Charles told me that his wife was cold and unresponsive. I listened carefully and patiently for a few sessions, offering empathy and trying to encourage him to express his frustration. Of course, I knew that I was hearing only his side of the story and imagined that Sherry likely had another angle on things. After several weeks of laying out his position, Charles finally said, "Okay, Doc, so we know what's happening here. Now tell me what to do." I paused briefly, and then, in the most non-accusatory way I could, said, "I think you need to work harder on yourself." As you might imagine, this did not elicit a very positive response. Let's just say Charles expressed that he'd been wasting his time and money coming to see me.

Bill and Tammy were the parents of Jennifer, a recent high school graduate. They were heartbroken over the disrespectful ways Jennifer was behaving the summer before she left for college. I listened, empathized and explained to them that some of this behavior may have been Jennifer's way of separating from them by injecting distance into their relationship. Bill and Tammy were incredulous that Jennifer could be so ungrateful and wanted me to suggest ways of bringing her "back in line." They wanted me to offer strategies—removing privileges or threatening to refuse to pay for college, for example—they might use to get Jennifer to behave more appropriately. I listened, but encouraged none of this. So, when they asked what they should do, I said, "I think you need to work harder on yourselves." They protested. "No, Doc, you haven't been listening. She's the one who's disrespectful. Why would we need to work on ourselves?" What they didn't yet understand was that the Principle of the Harvest suggested to me that, to some degree, Bill and Tammy were reaping what they'd sown. Had they been disrespectful of Jennifer, too? I thought it likely. And I thought it equally likely that if they would be more respectful toward her, over time, she would assume a more respectful attitude toward them.

A 40-year-old businessman named Ray told me that his new company had failed and he thought he was going to have to file for bankruptcy. Now, I'm not a financial adviser, by any stretch of the imagination. Ray was not coming for financial advice, but rather to deal with his feelings of failure, loss and depression. Again, I listened. I reflected on his situation, as he described it, and he agreed that I understood the details, thereby confirming that I was accurately understanding and empathizing with his plight. I asked specific questions about his financial assets and liabilities, and discovered that the lifestyle he'd adopted was well beyond his means, even before his business failed. I explored the options with him and then, when he seemed interested in my take on things, I said, "I think you ought to worker harder on yourself than anything else and reconsider whether you have to file for bankruptcy." Rather that being upset with me, Ray was one of those patients who was actually interested in what I saw in his predicament, and actually started to work himself out of it.

Andrea came to me complaining about her boss. It was clear she wanted a pass out of her department, and her ulterior motive in coming to me was the hope that I would write a letter to her employer's human resources department recommending that she be moved. Imagine her dismay when I suggested, after weeks of "hearing her out," that I thought the solution was not moving to another department, but taking it upon herself to work hard on what she could do differently. Oh, she was not happy with me. But she did keep coming, and as she improved herself, her situation at work improved, too.

Who's It All About?

Good news! It really *is* all about *you*, after all!

Humans have an incredible propensity for seeing themselves as the center of the universe. I'm here to tell you that it's true: The world does revolve around you....

Well, not exactly. Let's say that it's true that *your* world revolves around you. But you can't ever mistake *your* world for *the* world. Because *the* world is very little about you, no matter who you are.

There has been nothing that I've done in my clinical practice that has more frustrated patients than asking them to apply the Principle of the Common Denominator. When they first come to see me, they hate it, almost universally. But later, they thrive on it.

You see, the Principle of the Common Denominator says, "Work harder on yourself than on anything else, and everything in your life will get better." You, after all, are the common denominator to all of the problems in your life. So if *you* change, it only stands to reason that everything else will, too.

Before you conclude that I'm an insensitive or shallow-minded psychologist, think about this. First, I do listen and I do empathize. In other words, I demonstrate that I hear what my patients are saying, understand their circumstances and respect their feelings. Second, rather than promoting the notion that the problem is outside of them, leaving them to think that what really has to change to make their lives better is beyond their scope of power, I promote the truth that they are empowered to change everything and anything in their lives. I mean, after all: who better to change your financial situation, your health problems, your relationship issues or your work problems than you?

Of course, other people or situations sometimes cause significant problems in people's lives. Sometimes, the best thing is to leave an abusive spouse, hospitalize an unruly adolescent, file for bankruptcy or resign from a job. But these are the exceptions and solutions of last resort. And every one of them also involves an action *you* take: *you* leave an abusive spouse, *you* hospitalize an unruly adolescent, etc. So, even when the circumstances are dire and others are directly involved, you are *still* the common denominator. It really *is* all about you.

WHO's in *Control (of What)*?

What do you really control? I'm not sure anyone has the definitive answer to that question. But one thing is certain: You certainly *don't* control other people. The beginning and end of your empowerment appears to be yourself and the tasks for which you're responsible. Otherwise, you're really not in control.

Over the years, I've found that this idea is an affront to many people's sensibilities. The ability to be in control of events beyond ourselves and those tasks for which we are responsible seems to be a widespread misconception. On many occasions, I've gotten reactions of shock and outrage from parents when I've told their troublesome teens, in front of Mom and Dad, of course, that, after the age of about 14, their parents really are not in control. If you don't believe me, ask any 14-year-old if he can't get his hands on just about anything he wants or do whatever he chooses, whenever he wants to do it. Don't fool yourself: he can.

Parents aren't the only ones who don't like to face the truth of the Principle of the Common Denominator. I was once fired by a client in a medium-sized company when I told the management staff that they really couldn't control how hard their employees worked. I told them about discretionary effort and I talked about how their true power lay in influencing—not managing—their employees. No doubt they felt threatened by the very idea that they weren't really in control.

But all I'm saying is what everyone, at some level, already knows. Deceiving yourself will only make the situation worse—and truly does leave you powerless. You bring unnecessary anxiety on yourself if you believe you have to actually control someone who can't be controlled.

And so the game is on. How many teens or young adults have rebelled in order to prove this subtle, unspoken, but obvious truth? How much discretionary effort is lost each day because employees are treated as if they aren't really in control when, in fact, they *are* in control, and they know it—and, out of frustration with and disrespect for this sort of treatment, decide to lie down on the job? When you try to exert control you don't have, rebellion, whether passive or aggressive or passive/aggressive, is the order of the day. You manage only yourself, and realizing the truth of the Principle of the Common Denominator frees you from the desperate and fruitless act of trying to manage something you simply can't control.

The good news is that, when you embrace the Principle of the Common Denominator, you're empowered to direct your energy to the places in your life where you really can have impact. You can work on yourself, and you can change if you want to. You can inspire others in your life to be more responsible for their own behavior, as well. The Principle of the Common Denominator doesn't say that you don't have influence. You just don't have control over anyone's actions but your own. So, if you really want to change something, you'd better begin with you.

It's MANAGEABLE

So, why are people so hesitant to work on themselves? In my experience, it's because they don't want to believe that they are the solution to their problems—or, if they're convinced they *are* the problem, they don't know where to start. The prospect of change is overwhelming.

But, as the Principle of the Common Denominator suggests, "if you are not the problem, then there is no solution." This is actually an empowering statement. Whatever your circumstance, whatever your problem, *you* are the solution or there is no solution. The Principle of the Common Denominator actually works hand in hand with the Principle of the Harvest: *you* determine your harvest, based on what you're planting right now.

Where to start is a tougher issue, but it's not as overwhelming as it seems. In fact, right now, there are only four to six things that you need to work on that would make 80 percent of the difference in your life.[45] This is a variation on the Rule of 80/20, which says, for example, that 80 percent of a company's business comes from 20 percent of its customers. Take care of that 20 percent of customers, and the great majority of your business will be solid. Similarly, you may think you have 25 or 30 things in your life that need work—and maybe you do. But if you choose four to six of them—the four to six that seem biggest and most critical—you'll be surprised at how much your life improves. Some of those other problems may improve or disappear, too.

That's right: just four to six. Of course, these are four to six significant things. Each one may touch upon several different areas of your life. But the number of things you really need to work on is still between four and six. And working on these four to six things will make 80 percent of the difference in your life.

That's a huge improvement. Most people who make an 80 percent improvement are so much better off that they find it much easier to deal with the remaining 20 percent of their problems.

For example, I've had many patients who have relationship issues across the board. They've had multiple marriages. They have great difficulty in work relationships. They have poor relationships with their kids. It becomes clear to me, almost invariably, that these people have issues with respect. It's certainly true that they are not respected by their significant others. But it's also true that they have not been respectful. So, when we deal with the details of respectful relationships and I encourage them to be more respectful to others in their lives, several of their problems improve.

In fact, one of the best ways to determine the four to six things you need to work on is to look at what you dislike about your life. Again, you can clearly see the intersection between the Principle of the Common

Denominator and the Principle of the Harvest:
if you don't like the harvest, you change the planting.
You change the planting.

It's simple; but it's not easy. I've come to realize
that everything that is best for us is difficult. As Mihaly
Csikszentmihalyi says, 'the things that lead to a sense of
well-being in life, home and work are those things that
require us to stretch ourselves.' The sense of well-being
comes from delaying gratification and expending effort.
The easy stuff—the quick gratification—brings pleasure,
but is generally, in the long run, a disaster.

Another way to determine the four to six things
you need to work on is to consider what you do well,
but haven't been doing enough of. In other words,
what strengths could you focus on that would make the
greatest difference in your life? All too often, we focus
on problems and weaknesses to the exclusion of our
strengths. It's easy to imagine how focusing on what we
do best would have a widespread and profound effect
on our daily life experience.

Consider the things you don't like about your life and
look at what they have in common. Consider what you
do well, but perhaps have been neglecting. Start working
harder on yourself in these areas. It's only four to six
things. It's manageable.

It's *Contagious!*

Not that it should matter—because, according to the
Principle of the Common Denominator, we shouldn't be
too worried about what others do—but this strategy of
working on yourself is contagious. You see, every one of
us is looking for someone who has an idea of where he
or she is going. It's human nature to be insecure and to
imitate those who seem to have the answers.

A few years ago, quite spontaneously, I decided to
climb the stairs to my office every day for a year. So,
beginning January 1, I climbed the eight flights of stairs
every time I arrived at my office building. Some days,
I climbed the stairs only once in the morning, when I
came to work. But other days, if I left the building to go
to the hospital to see a patient or do a consult or to
attend a meeting or go to lunch, I'd climb the stairs
two or three times in a day. Except for just a few times
that year, when I was carrying too many things to make
climbing reasonable, I kept my pledge to myself and I
climbed those stairs.

The most interesting thing happened. On several
occasions, I entered the office huffing and puffing,
out of breath because I'd just climbed the stairs. And
on more than a few occasions, my office staff and my
patients saw see me panting and asked why. I'd explain

that, as long as I was coming up eight flights, I might as well get my heart rate up. After all, it was good for me. You know: the Principle of the Harvest.

By the end of that year, at least three of my employees —and even a couple of my patients—were regularly climbing the stairs. In fact, although my stair-climbing year is several years in the past, I have a former patient who will still climb the stairs to see if I have a minute to visit. He says, "I was in the area and thought I needed a little exercise, so I came to climb the stairs and see you."

Please understand: I never told anyone, not one person, that he should climb the stairs. I never even implied that anyone should climb the stairs. I had no intention of influencing anyone else to do anything. I just did it. I worked on myself, and it was contagious.

The *Second* PRINCIPLE at Work in Your *Organization*

When I say, "Work harder on yourself than on anything else and everything else in your life will get better," a part of why I believe everything else will get better is that others see what you're doing and are compelled to work on themselves, too. I don't think that's the reason you should begin to work on yourself, but I do think that is part of the reason things improve. When you show people that *you* are empowered and working to make a difference in your own life, they realize that they're empowered, too.

And imagine the effect that living by this principle has on an organization. Imagine that the organization's leaders focus on their only true power to change. As that focus spreads to those around them, the culture of the organization reflects a new and powerful dynamic: that the solution to all of each individual's problems lies with him, and the solution to all of our problems lies with us. Once that idea permeates an organization, there are no market forces that can stop it. It's really easy to do—and it's also so easy not to do. And that's why it is uncommon sense.

Get PHILOSOPHICAL

If you really think about it, working on yourself harder than you work on anything else is a daunting task. You have 168 hours in a week. If you sleep eight hours a night, you spend a third of your available hours sleeping. Of the 112 hours left, you spend a little more than another third working and nearly a quarter on personal maintenance: showering, eating, brushing your teeth, etc. When you have to devote so much time to the necessary and routine tasks of your life, it can be tough to find the time to work harder on yourself than on anything else. It's easy to see why, even if you agree with the Principle of the Common Denominator, you have a tough time implementing it.

But then, we can work on ourselves while at work and in our personal time. In fact, for many of us, working on ourselves involves eating better, getting more exercise, generally taking better care of ourselves, and working with more focus. What this really requires is not just a change in behavior, but also a change in perspective. You must have a *philosophy*: a considered approach to how you live your life in almost every activity, at almost every moment. It's an increased awareness of what you're doing and how you're doing it; and it's the only way that you can truly work harder on yourself than anything else.

So, create a plan. Write a manifesto. Make your first step a philosophical one. Make your intentions clear to yourself. Tell yourself—and remind yourself—about your philosophy of life and what you want to do *right now*, in this minute, to make the most of it. You'll see that you really *do* have the time. In fact, time is *all you have*.

I hope that, at this point, you're seeing that there is a reality behind the everyday reality. There's a Principle of the Harvest that can help you see the consequences of your actions. And you're empowered to change your life in positive ways because of the Principle of the Common Denominator. Remember: just four to six things can make all the difference in the world...well, 80 percent of the difference, anyway.

Now there's another uncommon sense principle that you need to consider. And it's a big one—so big that it's known as the *Supreme Principle of the Universe.*

The *Second* Principle
SUMMARIZED

- The Principle of the Common Denominator says, "Work harder on yourself than on anything else, and everything in your life will get better."

- The beginning and end of your empowerment appears to be yourself and the tasks for which you're responsible. Otherwise, you're really not in control.

- The Principle of the Common Denominator suggests, "If you are not the problem, then there is no solution."

- There are only four to six things that you need to work on that would make 80 percent of the difference in your life.

- When you show people that *you* are empowered and working to make a difference in your own life, they realize that they're empowered, too.

- You must have a *philosophy*: a considered approach to how you live your life in almost every activity, at almost every moment. It's an increased awareness of what you're doing and how you're doing it, and it's the only way that you can truly work harder on yourself than anything else.

THE THIRD
UNIVERSAL PRINCIPLE
OF UNCOMMON SENSE

THE SUPREME PRINCIPLE

OF THE UNIVERSE:

ENTROPY

happens

AGELESS

Paul is in his mid-80s. He's spry. To say he's active is to understate the level of activity he maintains. I've heard men 50 years his junior marvel at his energy and strength. To hear him on the phone, his voice with so much energy, he could easily pass for 40.

When you see him, you know he's an octogenarian. He's gray and he's wrinkled. He walks slowly and with care, especially after dark, knowing that a fall could be not only painful, but could also lead to a prolonged convalescence. In many ways, Paul is just like others his age; yet, there is something decidedly different about him. What is it?

Paul is a simple man living a simple life, but he's not simplistic. He's lived in the same house for decades, even though he can afford more and bigger accommodations. When you ask him why he and his wife never moved, he says, "Never thought of it." Yet, he's one of the brightest, most mentally active men I know.

And it's not that he hasn't accomplished a great deal. He has. His career was notable and his accomplishments breathtaking, yet these facts are not what cause him to stand apart from his peers. The difference is not that obvious. But what is it?

One thing is certain: Paul has always taken good care of himself. He's eaten right and worked hard. The adage "use it or you lose it" seems to have been Paul's motto. His physical vitality is testament to the benefit of "using it." And Paul has always read a lot, too. Same principle, I think. This may explain why he's so cognitively astute. But what of this sense about him that he defies the inevitable effects of aging? Even as his senses dull and his body weakens, he grows in strength of joy and enthusiasm for life. What about this?

And as I experience Paul, I wonder what I can learn from him. The importance of staying active, both physically and mentally—I'll remember that. But what else does he know that I need to know?

It all seems to come back to simplicity. Clearly, a good part of Paul's youthfulness is born of the freedom of his simplicity. And simplicity is tough for me. It's hard not to get caught up in wanting, even believing I need, all of the trappings of our culture. But the more I observe Paul, the more certain I am that these things only complicate life. They distract us from what is more important.

Simplicity. How can I simplify my life and remain simple? What can I consider here and now that will allow me the experience of life Paul is having in his mid-80s? Maybe the real question is, what is it beyond his active and simple lifestyle that keeps Paul young in spirit? What's the thing that drives him to stay physically and mentally active? How can he be so contented with such simplicity? This unnamed, intangible characteristic: this is what I would like to understand.

Because wanting more would seem to be common sense. So, this must be uncommon sense....

We *All* FALL *Down*

The Supreme Principle of the Universe is entropy: the inherent and inevitable, relentless process of deterioration, disintegration, decay and disorder.[46] Entropy is the most difficult of these universal, uncommon-sense principles to acknowledge. We don't like to think about the universe deteriorating. After all, our bodies are part of the universe. So, the Supreme Principle of the Universe means that we're going to die: all of us. Entropy affects every created thing and everybody.

Bummer, eh? But, lest you think this is a negative message, I'm here to tell you that the real danger of the Supreme Principle of the Universe lies not in recognizing it, but ignoring it.

We accept that anything that has a beginning most certainly has an end, and is, therefore, subject to entropy. Entropy is the increasing likelihood that the original order within any creation or system will, over time, gradually become more and more disordered. Entropy is the process of aging, and it's a natural, universal process.

We are, in a clinical sense, created systems. (This has nothing to do with your belief or disbelief in a higher power. It's a matter of physical reality: your mother and father came together and created you.) The process of aging and, ultimately death, are the inevitable consequences of entropy. As we go through our lives, we gradually experience greater and greater disorder in our physical and mental being, which is manifested in what we refer to as disease.

And while entropy is a reality in our life experience, it's not necessarily part of our experience of life. What this means is that while entropy is gradually taking its toll on us, we are not, on a day-to-day basis, aware of its insidious effects.

No one doubts the aging process and no one doubts the increasing prevalence of disease as we age. Nor do we doubt the inevitability of death of all living systems. But we sure do live in denial. Most days, in some if not many ways, we live as if The Supreme Principle of the Universe somehow doesn't apply to us.

COMPLEXITY & *Entropy*

The Supreme Principle of the Universe has a lot in common with Murphy's Law. It's not exactly that if something can go wrong, it will; not everything goes wrong. But it is true that the more things there are that *can* go wrong, the more likely it is that one *will* go wrong. In other words, the more complicated the system, the greater the entropy.[47]

An example might help. Let's say I have a full deck of 52 playing cards arranged by suit and numerical order—which, for the purposes of this example, I'll call the deck's proper and original order. I throw them up in the air, then pick them all up again. The likelihood that the cards would be back in their original order after I've tossed them and retrieved them is far less than the likelihood that they would be in a new and different order. The cards are now in *disorder.* This is an example of high entropy.

Now, let's say I begin with only the hearts from the deck of playing cards. I have only 13 cards. If I did the same thing—threw them in the air and picked them up—it's still likely that they would not be in the original order. But there are fewer disordered possibilities and the chances of the original order reappearing are greatly increased. This is low entropy.

You can apply this same thinking to everything from playing a piece of music to baking a cake to executing a triple axel. The greater the complexity, the greater the likelihood that whatever you're attempting won't come together in the right order.

Which is why we thrill to the beauty of a proficient performance of Mozart and then marvel at the baker who can create a delicate Hummingbird cake and admire the skater who can make complex spins and leaps seem effortless. We love to "beat" entropy by pulling off the complex. Perhaps it helps us believe, temporarily, that we can master the inherent and the inevitable. But, as a rule, "it's not nice to fool Mother Nature." Entropy is inherent in the experience of all created things, including living things, and it is relentless. In the end, arrogantly ignoring entropy leads to disaster, always. Make no mistake about it, be under no illusion: entropy always wins.

Entropy in our daily lives can be so subtle as to be nearly invisible. I've had corporate executives—bright, well-educated, accomplished people—say they don't believe in entropy. To me, that seems like not believing in gravity. But just like gravity, entropy is so ubiquitous that it "goes without thinking" most of the time. And that's the point. That's why acknowledging it is "uncommon sense."

Physicians believe in entropy: they see its effects all the time. Insurance underwriters know of entropy: their actuarial tables are based on the assumption of entropy. Even automakers and other manufacturers write warranties based on the expectation and prediction of the rate of entropy. The fact of entropy is actually built into and accounted for in every aspect of our lives. It just "goes without saying."

Entropy is also at the root of our experience of disappointment. As entropy has its insidious effect through disease and disorder, our life experience can become one of frustration and despair. Acknowledging the reality of entropy in our life experience brings more realistic expectations and less room for disappointment. It can also help us awaken to the fact that, although entropy is part of our life experience, it doesn't have to be part of our experience of life.

Put it all together and, if we would truly acknowledge the reality of the Supreme Principle of the Universe, we would seek simplicity in our lives.

Entropy, Anguish *&* NEGENTROPY

Remember our old nemesis, anguish? You'll recall that anguish is not a feeling; rather, it's background experience that is like a layer of distressing misery underneath everything in your life. You can actually feel happy and still have an underlying experience of anguish. You can also be anxious and depressed and have the experience of anguish. It's there, regardless of your fleeting feelings. And it is nagging.

Anguish is the sense that, in some way, you are pitted against yourself, fragmented and out of sync.[48] And of course, if you are in denial of the Supreme Principle of the Universe, you are *way* out of sync. If you deny or ignore entropy, it can deepen the experience of anguish.

There's another interesting way in which entropy is related to anguish. Anguish is the belief that something is wrong, that something is missing, that you will lose or have already lost something. The reality of entropy is an insidious loss or losing. Because of this connection, anguish can actually be a help in your life. If you attend to the experience of anguish, it can bring awareness of the Supreme Principle of the Universe and alert you to the daily challenge of slowing entropy.

All of life is a struggle in this effort to slow entropy, which is a process Csikszentmihalyi calls *negentropy*.[49] Many of the things we do every day, without even thinking about them, are intended to retard the process of entropy. We brush our teeth to slow the process of tooth and gum decay. We bathe and clean our clothes to get rid of dirt and grime. All hygiene is actually negentropy.

Then, there are more disciplined things we do to fight the continuous effects of atrophy, another form of entropy. We exercise. We eat right. We take on mental challenges. We actively build negentropy into our lives— the more the better.

And what about negentropy with our possessions? After all, they, too, are created and are, therefore, subject to entropy. So, we get the oil in our car changed regularly to slow the gradual and destructive effects of engine friction. We paint the wood exterior of the house to beautify and protect. These are efforts to fight entropy. When you think about it, we spend as much time each day dealing with the prospect and consequences of entropy as we spend with productive activity.

There are two keys, then to negentropy: an awareness and acceptance of entropy, and persistence in the effort to slow its effects. So, many of life's problems are caused by unawareness or denial of entropy, or of failing to embrace negentropy diligently and consistently. The consequences are devastating—not just to individuals, but to organizations, as well.

Organizational
ENTROPY

An individual is relatively simple. An organization is not. So, it's no wonder that entropy is a threat to organizations —by which I mean any group of people: corporations, churches, communities and families. It's long been taken as fact that all organizations of any type have lifecycles, just as individuals do. Organizations are continually in the process of decay and disorganization, leading eventually to disorder. It is accurate to say that the difference between corporations, or even families, that survive and thrive versus those that ultimately dissolve, is the effectiveness with which they deal with the insidiousness of organizational entropy.

And, of course, the more complex the organization,

the greater the threat of entropy; the more that can go wrong, the more that will go wrong. Likewise, the greater your awareness of the presence of entropy and the more persistent you are in addressing it, the more effective you'll be in slowing or minimizing organizational entropy's effect.

When you really give this some thought, the concept of organizational entropy explains a lot of things. For example, your company might grow to a size and a level of complexity that interferes with its ability to sustain acceptable levels of profitability. In the attempt to gain economy of scale and diversify, an organization actually invites a higher level of entropy that's barely noticeable in the short run; but, in the long run, can be malignant. As we've experienced time and time again, the remedy is often divesting the company of those things that once seemed to be reasonable attempts to diversify in order to return the company to its core competencies. Indeed, if corporate restructuring is *not* aimed at simplifying, the results are usually futile.

In families, too, complexity is a bane to survival. Parents need to be more respectful of the effects of entropy on a family's ability to function under the load of too many possessions, too many activities, and too many distractions. The 56-percent divorce rate in this country is, to some degree, attributable to this sort of organizational complexity and its accelerating effects on entropy. In families, such traditions as family dinners, vacations and gatherings at holidays are routine, persistent efforts in negentropy.

Time is also a factor in entropy; systems do get increasingly complex over time. Whether you're talking about a corporation, a community or a family, it appears that complexity is inevitable.

So, organizational simplicity is not about staying small or avoiding opportunity to diversify, or running in place. That would not be simplicity, but *simplistic*. It was Oliver Wendell Holmes who noted that "there is little value in simplicity this side of complexity, but great value of simplicity that is on the other side of complexity." It's simplistic to avoid complexity, which is often necessary for growth and even survival. Simplicity, on the other hand, is looking past the simple to the complex, then past the complex in a way that allows you to return to the simple.

Simple. *Complex.* Simple.

In the beginning of the Family, there was the Couple. And the Family was fruitful and multiplied, and instead of the Couple alone, there were Children. And if the Couple was especially blessed (or especially crazy), there were two or three or four or even more Children....

And the simple little family system becomes increasingly complicated. There are more chores to be done, a bigger home, more dinners to fix, more interests to satisfy, more schedules to accommodate, more homework, more college educations to finance. Yet, if the leaders in the family understand the significant destructive influence of high entropy, they will look to lead simply by looking to simply lead. This means that, rather than attempting to manage everyone's life experience, they are more concerned with leading their family in such a way as to encourage the best experience of life, whatever that is.

I know a family of seven, the Tomlinsons, that has a rule, largely out of necessity, that no child can be involved in more than one extracurricular activity. You may think the parents are lazy or don't want to be very involved with their children, or that they're so overwhelmed that they simply can't manage a family of this size. But note that, in part because of the lack of complexity in the family's schedule, they are frequently known to get out of bed on a non-school morning and just start driving toward some little-known place of interest. The whole Tomlinson clan—all seven of them. These day trips are traditions that have become part of a powerful adhesive that binds this family together.

The Tomlinsons experienced increasing complexity with the growth of their family. But they've focused on the simple by leading their family to a better experience of life, rather than trying to provide a better life experience. They're doing what, as you might remember, a friend of mine mentioned as being "more important to prepare your children for the road than the road for your children."

In their efforts to manage their kids' life experiences, too many parents run themselves ragged. But the fact is, through their leadership, they could provide their child with a much better experience of life. This is the simplicity that is on the other side of complexity.

The challenge dealing with the Supreme Principle of the Universe is to keep leading simple. Of course, keeping the organization simple is also a hedge against a higher level of entropy. But keeping leadership simple is the most reasonable, practical and workable approach. Remember: organizations will necessarily become complex; leadership doesn't have to.

We Have Met the *Enemy,* AND IT IS US

When you consider the Supreme Principle of the Universe, it's clear that the enemy is not "out there." It's not the competition, or the market conditions, or that one bad seed spoiling everything. The enemy is within—and, in fact, the enemy is actually at its most powerful when we *believe* it's outside of ourselves. To believe that we manage anything but ourselves is to take our eye off the ball; to simplify and manage that which is manageable—

nothing but ourselves—is to realistically address the issue of entropy in our own lives.

(I think you can also begin to see here how the Supreme Principle of the Universe is related to the Principle of the Common Denominator and, by extension, the Principle of the Harvest. You have to embrace the principle of entropy by working on yourself—and you will reap what you sow. It's really that simple.)

The greatest threat to your organization comes from within. It's the relentless grind of entropy. The market is demanding and competition can be fierce, but time after time, business leaders tell me that the greatest threat their company faces is from within. Sometimes, they call it "complacency." Sometimes, they call it "labor dispute." Sometimes, they call it "poor product development" or "lack of innovation" or "problems motivating my people." They can call it whatever they want. By any name, they're dealing with the fragmentation of their organizations' functioning that is the result of the ongoing work of the Supreme Principle of the Universe.

COOPERATION *vs.* *Competition*

Our capitalist economy in America has always been, and continues to be, based on the notion that competition is a good thing. It *is* a good thing—at least for consumers. Competition in a free market keeps quality high and prices honest.

But there's recently been an increasing challenge to the idea that competition is good *inside* organizations.[50] In fact, it has long been understood that competition within an organization leads to demoralization by virtue of the fact that someone wins, but others lose. The people who lose are demoralized and, with demoralization in its ranks, the organization loses. This type of intra-organizational competitiveness actually leads to decreased loyalty, increased employee turnover and, since employee retention is the best predictor of customer satisfaction, decreased customer satisfaction. So, competition within the ranks is a losing proposition.

Within certain types of organizations, competition is clearly undesirable. Social and religious groups may have competition within their ranks, but certainly not by conscious design. And families are dysfunctional to whatever degree competition exists among its members. In these organizations, cooperation—not competition— is encouraged.

But what about competition in the marketplace— that is, competition with competitors? Surely, that's okay.

Actually, this sort of competition may also be unwise. Remember, the economic times are changing. As we continue to transition from the Industrial Age with its manufacturing-based economy to the Information Age with a knowledge-based economy, competition may actually be an accelerant to entropy.

The Information Age causes us to challenge the wisdom of competition because of a concept referred to as the *social inhibition effect.*[51] This concept says that as processes become more cognitively challenging, or demand more creativity, competition actually undermines and inhibits the quality of a person's work. Competition stifles cognitive agility.

As long as tasks are well learned and well rehearsed, as they are in Industrial Age assembly-line production, there is a *social facilitation effect* of competition. Survival in the Industrial Age is based on the cost of production and pricing, so competing for greater efficiency through better processes and methods makes sense.

But while production and efficiency are still essential, the increasing maturity of production processes makes innovation and creativity—new ideas—even more important than cranking up the production methods. It's more important to do new things rather than just do things better.

This relates directly to discretionary effort. The greatest efficiencies are not found in better technology or better systems, but in accessing that 40 to 50 percent discretionary effort in your workforce.

And how is that done? In a word: cooperation.

Cooperation is the lesson of organizational entropy. Within the ranks of your organization, cooperation brings greater connectedness, more passion, greater loyalty and more stability. When you focus on internal cooperation and accessing discretionary effort, you're embracing the Supreme Principle of the Universe and addressing entropy, the greatest threat to your organization. By focusing energy on negentropy within the organization, it only stands to reason that there is necessarily less energy and attention to be focused on competition in the marketplace.

I'm not saying that organizations don't have to concern themselves with competition. You most definitely have to keep an eye on the market. I'm saying only that it's far less important than it has been in the past. Focus on what you can control, and what happens in the marketplace will take care of itself.

Personal IMMUNITY from *Entropy*

Whether we acknowledge entropy as a reality or not, we likely engage efforts to immunize ourselves against entropy. The degree to which we acknowledge entropy will drive our effort to immunize ourselves. And, just as with organizational entropy, the keys to personal immunity from entropy are negentropy and simplicity.

As I've mentioned, our negentropy efforts include such everyday activities as hygiene, proper diet and exercise.

Many medical treatments and procedures are aimed at negentropy; for example, Vytorin helps to control cholesterol and, therefore, slows heart disease. We have knees repaired not only so we'll have less discomfort, but also so we can stay active, because we all know that inactivity leads to higher entropy. "Use it or lose it" is actually a statement about entropy.

How about simplicity? For many people, simplicity begins with prioritization. We all know "we can only do so much", which is another common, yet indirect, acknowledgement of the process of entropy. Prioritization simplifies and decreases the likelihood of disorder in our lives. Setting limits and boundaries are also efforts toward simplification. Not only do we need to know what's most important, but also within our priorities, how much we can do.

And just as with organizational immunity from entropy, we as individuals need to recognize that the real threat we face in life comes mostly from within and is mostly the result of the Supreme Principle of the Universe. Your focus on the circumstances you face, or the people who frustrate you, is far less effective in helping you lead a life than working on negentropy and simplification.

Is *Anything* ENTROPY-PROOF?

Negentropy and simplification cannot ultimately negate entropy. Entropy is an inevitable process in all created things. All things with a beginning and an end must deal with the Supreme Principle of the Universe. But what of uncreated things? And what is uncreated? Is there anything in the human experience that has no beginning and no end?

To my way of thinking—and to the way of thinking of more than 90 percent of the world's population—the answer is a resounding "yes." Most people believe there is a central part of what you are that, for all we can tell, has no beginning and no end. That part of you is what the world of religion calls *soul* or *spirit* and the world of psychology calls *consciousness*. There is, to date, no evidence that we ever lose consciousness. Even when "unconscious," as in a coma or under anesthetic, people often report that they experienced what was going on around them. They still have consciousness.

In the last few decades, as medical science has improved its ability to resuscitate people from a state that can really be referred to only as "death", there has been a growing volume of reports of near-death experiences. People say they experience a change in consciousness, but not a loss of consciousness. Their "new" consciousness includes seeing a bright light, passing through a tunnel and, in some reports, seeing family members and friends who have already passed away.

Of course, our faith traditions have always told us of the spirit and the soul. If you really think about it, it's unlikely that you'd disagree that the human spirit is critically important to your experience of life. Some would claim this invisible, immeasurable element of human experience is the single most important aspect of most life situations.

Perhaps consciousness should not be understood as soul or spirit itself, but rather as the human experience of spirit.[52] But whatever you call it, however you describe it, one thing is sure: there is an intangible aspect of all individuals that gives them their essence. With it, you are alive and unique. Without it, you are only a shell.

When I lost my long-time friend and business partner, Steve, I couldn't help but think about consciousness and spirit. I realized that if I had a choice between having him back, alive, before my eyes in physical form, but without his spirit, or I could have his spirit and never see his physical form again, I'd most definitely choose to experience his spirit and forgo the physical. I'd prefer both, but I'd gladly settle for Steve's spirit. That is what I miss so much.

Consciousness *Is*

We have much less information about the origins of our personal consciousness than we do about virtually anything else in our lives. We don't know when consciousness starts—if, in fact, it even has a beginning. But for the sake of this discussion, let's consider the possibility that, since we have no evidence of the end of consciousness, then we have no evidence that it actually begins. Consciousness simply is.

This is an affront to our rational way of thinking. Consciousness simply *is*? Surely, we can't put our trust in something that just *is*, can we?

Well, we do. In every day and in every way, we absolutely trust our consciousness as the essence of what we are. Your consciousness is the "you" that observes everything—the "you" that observes not only what's exterior to yourself, but your thoughts and emotions, as well. It's not an easy concept, but stay with me for a minute.

Think about the book you're reading right now. It has a certain weight, a certain size. Words on the page—you can see and describe those. You can also describe your hands holding the book and your behavior of reading and of turning pages. *You* are not your hands, and *you* are not the act of reading. In a way, your hands are like the book, which you may even describe as *your* book.

Now, consider what you're thinking and feeling.

You may be thinking, "I wish he'd get on with this", or "I don't really get it" or "I need a candy bar." You may be feeling enlightened or irritated or bored. So, you can observe and describe your thoughts and feelings— and so *your thoughts and feelings are not* you. By definition, something you observe is exterior to you.

So, "you" are not your body. "You" are not what you do. "You" are not what you think or feel. So, who or what is the "you" who is reading this sentence?

I can't describe that. Whoever or whatever is doing the observing is, by definition, beyond my observation; if it were not, then it would simply be another object of a perceiver, wouldn't it? In other words, the "you" that perceives your thoughts is a perceiver who never is seen and cannot be observed—not by you, at least. This is the *real* you: your consciousness.

And that brings me to the point. If there is any immunity from entropy, it is in our consciousness, our spirit. In fact, entropy does not exist in consciousness, because consciousness has no beginning and no end. When you are awakened to your consciousness, you're not minimizing or slowing the process of entropy, as you can do in your physical existence though negentropy efforts and by simplifying. You're actually stepping outside the world of entropy.

The *Third* PRINCIPLE at Work in Your *Organization*

So, what about organizations? Do they have consciousness? Is there any such thing as organizational immunity from entropy?

If you consider my definition of consciousness as the *human experience of spirit*, then, most definitely, organizations have consciousness: no one would doubt that organizations have spirit. These days, organizational spirit is often referred to as "corporate culture." Whatever you call it, you're talking about the essence of the company—and an invaluable ingredient in its success.

So, if an organization has a spirit, is it, like the human spirit, free of entropy? Of course it is. In the same way that an individual's consciousness is outside that realm of entropy, so is an organization's spirit. But the organization, just like the individual, must choose to "live" in its consciousness rather than in those aspects of itself that are subject to entropy—that is, if the organization desires to gain immunity from entropy.

Unfortunately, most organizations—again, like most people—attempt to manage their life experience rather than live their experience of life. They choose to fight against entropy rather than step out of the realm of entropy. It's a fight they can wage for a while, but it's not a fight they can win. Negentropy and simplicity are two useful strategies for dealing with the inevitable organizational entropy. But they provide no immunity from entropy.

The oldest organization in the world, the family, is primarily focused on consciousness or spirit. In healthy, strong families, relationships are paramount. Strong families see beyond behavior, thought, belief and emotion, and embrace their members at a deeper, spiritual level, appreciating a greater purpose. The stronger the consciousness or spirit of the family, the more immunity the family has from entropy.

The next oldest organizations in the world are religious institutions, and they, too, are focused on spirit. Our faith traditions have outlived every government, most countries, and most certainly every commercial endeavor known to man. Whatever your view of these groups, it is a fact that they seem to have life beyond the forces of entropy that affect most other institutions. And regardless of their internal controversies and problems, there is always an influential group of leaders within any surviving religious organization that focuses on the spiritual, especially in trying times. It is this focus that sustains them in the face of entropy.

Not-for-profit organizations show similar characteristics. They, too, if grounded in consciousness or spirit, show ability to rise above the typical organizational entropy and survive, even thrive, in spite of difficult times and events and the relentlessness of the Supreme Principle of the Universe.

So, what does this intangible preservative called spirit look like? And can it exist in any organization?

The answer is a resounding "yes": it can exist in any and all organizations. Remember that living from consciousness or spirit means seeing beyond that which is readily apparent. It's seeing beyond those things that most of us usually respond to: behavior, thoughts and emotions. It is seeing from a broader, grander and deeper perspective. And so, organizations living from spirit consider themselves to be serving a purpose greater than achieving any given outcome and certainly greater than primarily creating wealth for stockholders. They ask, "How can we give?" rather than, "What do we get?" They have leaders who understand that true leadership is about serving, not about being served. They always see what is hoped for, not what is feared. They act in service to the people they serve, always doing the right thing, regardless of the outcome. They see themselves with a long-term legacy, and this long view allows them freedom from a sense of urgency. They have stable, consistent focus. And as I've already said, they see people as their greatest asset.

In other words, organizational immunity from entropy has nothing to do with time management, quality control or focus on the bottom line. It has everything to do with inspiring and motivating people.

I know of an up-and-coming marketing company that has a 300-year vision. That's right: 300 years. Think about that: With that kind of perspective, your daily activities and decisions are unquestionably different than if every day is driven by short-term problem solving and profit margins. This company grows at a consistent, measured rate. Even more important, they have tremendous loyalty among their employees and clients. They have cutting-edge ideas and processes, but these aren't what set them apart in their field. It's their people, and their realization that their people are primary to their success.

Consider some other companies known for being "different": ServiceMaster®, Medtronic, Chick-fil-A®, The Toro Company, The Ritz-Carlton Hotel Company. I would suggest that what sets them apart from the competition is that they exercise their option for immunity from entropy. Each of these organizations lives by a spirit and values people themselves more than anything that can be directly observed.

Live *Conscious* of SIMPLICITY and in the SIMPLICITY of *Consciousness*

Let's recap. The Supreme Law of the Universe is entropy. Entropy is inherent and inevitable for all created things. The only effective way to combat entropy is through negentropy and simplicity. With simplicity, not only do you lower entropy, but also, by having more energy to spare, give yourself the ability to better sustain your negentropy efforts. For example, if you clear enough time in your busy schedule for a daily workout, you'll also have more energy to jog or lift weights or ride a bike.

Entropy is inherent and inevitable in our physical existence—but not to consciousness. Of all human experience, consciousness is the only aspect not subject to entropy. That's because consciousness, for all we know, is uncreated.

So, if all of this is true, what good is it?

First, many people live under the awful burden of perfection. Although they would adamantly claim that they know they can't be perfect, they live as if they don't know this. It puts them under tremendous pressure.

Identifying and living with an awareness of entropy can help you change the burdensome expectation of perfection to the idea of doing the best you can to slow the inevitable process of deterioration. In other words, admitting the presence of entropy is admitting the impossibility of perfection—and that's a good thing. If you don't have to be perfect, you're free to make mistakes, pick yourself up, dust yourself off and try again.

Second, in living with increased awareness of consciousness —of that part of yourself called spirit—you can live in the reality of wholeness. Perfection is a burden, but living with a knowledge that you are wholly and completely what you are supposed to be is a tremendous encouragement. There's no more need to struggle to be something you're not or something you can't ever be.

At some point, everyone is in anguish. At some point, everyone has to face the fact of entropy. It is, after all, the Supreme Law of the Universe. Wise leaders acknowledge and understand this uncommon sense idea and simplify what they can, engage in negentropy where they can, and consider the significance of consciousness in their daily lives.

And we've only just begun our discussion of consciousness. In fact, the rest of the uncommon-sense principles have something to say about this infrequently addressed, yet universally experienced, topic. Buckle up; it's going to be a wild ride. But it's going to be a lot of fun, too. And I promise there's a great payoff at the end.

The *Third* Principle
SUMMARIZED

- *The Supreme Principle of the Universe* is entropy: the inherent and inevitable, relentless process of deterioration, disintegration, decay and disorder.

- If we would truly acknowledge the reality of the Supreme Principle of the Universe, we would seek simplicity in our lives.

- There are two keys to combating the Supreme Principle of the Universe: an awareness and acceptance of entropy, and persistence in the effort to slow its effects.

- Organizations are continually in the process of decay and disorganization, leading eventually to disorder.

- The greater your awareness of the presence of entropy and the more persistent you are in addressing it, the more effective you'll be in slowing or minimizing organizational entropy's effect.

- As a leader, the challenge of dealing with the Supreme Principle of the Universe is to keep leading simple.

- The greatest threat to your organization comes from within. It's the relentless grind of entropy.

- Cooperation is the lesson of organizational entropy. Within the ranks of your organization, cooperation brings greater connectedness, more passion, greater loyalty and more stability.

- If there is any immunity from entropy, it is in our consciousness, our spirit. In fact, as far as we know, entropy does not exist in consciousness, because consciousness has no beginning and no end.

- Organizational immunity from entropy has nothing to do with time management, quality control or focus on the bottom line. It has everything to do with inspiring and motivating people.

- Ultimately, successful organizations live by a spirit and value people themselves more than anything that can be directly observed.

THE FOURTH
UNIVERSAL PRINCIPLE
OF UNCOMMON SENSE

THE EQUALIZER

PRINCIPLE:

HOW YOU *see*

IS WHAT YOU *see*

War STORIES

Ron was a powerful man, the CEO of a major corporation. Under Ron's guidance, the organization had become a multi-national juggernaut in its field. Of course, the board of directors had handsomely rewarded Ron with millions of dollars in compensation and tens of millions in stock options, which he exercised at their peak in value. As he approached retirement, it was obvious that he had accomplished all of his dreams for power and exceeded his wildest dreams for money.

At the height of Ron's business success, he and Gail, his wife of twenty years, were divorced. It was Ron's idea; Gail had not wanted the divorce, and appealed to Ron to keep the family together. There was no question that, over the years, Ron and Gail had grown apart. They had everything—big houses, fine cars and a wonderful lifestyle —but no friendship with each other.

In the end, the relationship was an arrangement. It hadn't started out that way, but it had ended up that way. A strong marriage had become a matter of convenience. There was no passion there—certainly not the sort of passion Ron was used to in his business life. So, Ron and Gail divorced, and Ron eventually remarried, to a woman fifteen years his junior.

Of course, in divorcing Gail, Ron also dramatically changed his relationship with his fifteen-year-old son,

Sean, and twelve-year-old daughter, Kayla. He did not see them nearly as much as he had when he was living at home. With his travel schedule, Ron was sometimes gone for weeks on end, so his kids were used to growing up without him. With his visitation schedule, Ron's time with his kids was well defined.

But something had changed. Sean and Kayla knew, beyond what they could verbally express, that their dad's priority was himself, then business, and that they were a distant third. They didn't doubt that he loved them—that wasn't the point—or that he'd drop everything if they were sick or injured. But short of an emergency, Sean and Kayla were afterthoughts in Ron's daily routine.

The kids also found that, once Ron remarried, they moved down one more notch. After all, Ron's new wife, Sally, was his "soul mate." The intensity of the romance of this new relationship was apparent to all.

When Ron retired, it was to a lifestyle only a few can afford. He lived on the Great Lakes in the summer and on the ocean in Florida in the winter. Of course, he traveled all over the world with Sally. Their relationship was good, but the romance had worn off, and Ron's life no longer offered the thrill of a "soul mate" that it had once seemed to promise. And what of the power that Ron had once enjoyed? Well, most of those he had interacted with on a daily basis for his whole career were "business associates." So, now that he was retired, when he called them—since he couldn't do anything for them or they for him—they often didn't return his calls. If they did, it felt to Ron like a courtesy call. Ron's relationships had been power based. With no formal power, he had no real friends. He became lonely and despondent.

And what of Sean and Kayla? Sean was married and starting his own family; Kayla was living and working in London. They were more involved with their mom than with Ron. They loved their dad, but didn't feel much connection with him.

What does a man do with himself at 72 years of age when he has no earthly power; his money can buy nothing bigger and better than he already has, and certainly nothing that will satisfy him emotionally; and the only deep relational connection he's experienced in the last twenty years was romantic, and it's long since passed? What does a man who has always thought himself capable of solving problems, one who is as competent in the things of practical life as most anyone alive, do when life seems empty and there doesn't seem to be the time to change course? What does a man do when he realizes that he's always depended on having the best life experiences, more power, more money, more excitement, in order to have the best experience of life—and now there are no life experiences that will any longer satisfy?

One April morning, Ron stepped into the garage at his posh Florida estate, stuck the barrel of his shotgun in his mouth, and blew off the back of his head. Ron had everything he'd ever wanted, and nothing he really needed.

Consider Ron's tragedy in light of Will's story. When
Will was 80 years old, he was more alive than when he
was 20. He had a kind of energy in his voice, a kind of
zest for life, that belied logic. Certainly, he had aged
physically and was continuing to age; no one escapes
the Supreme Principle of the Universe. Will's eyesight
gradually failed, his hearing diminished and, thanks
to his deteriorating hips, he had more difficulty getting
around. Every day was painful, to be sure. But Will never
complained—not because he willed himself to not
complain, but because he saw life from a different
perspective. Pain and pleasure occur in consciousness.
Our experience of pain and pleasure is determined by
our state of consciousness. To Will, life was not about
having the best daily life experiences, but rather having
the best experience of life, whatever the day might bring.

Will's uncommon-sense approach to living did not
start in his seventh decade of life, or even in his sixth.
Will began seeing the reality behind reality many decades
before his retirement, and his enthusiasm for life was a
consequence of his state of consciousness for many years.

Will, too, had been a CEO. His company was a
national firm of great renown: a leading-edge company
in a cutting-edge industry. When Will retired at age 65,
he, too, had millions of dollars and a very fine lifestyle.
Will, too, lived in the upper Midwest in the summer and
in the warm climate of Arizona, in the winter. Will, too,
had grown children—three daughters. Will, too, was

married to a woman that he thought, 53 years ago, was his "soul mate", if that's what the kids were calling them a half a century before.

But Will never counted on his life experiences to determine his experience of life. He never expected that more power or more money or more romance could, in any sustaining way, bring the best experience of life. Will was always more concerned about the type of person he was and having the best experience of whatever life brought his way than about his accomplishments or circumstances. For that reason, he had a deep and abiding friendship with his wife, Ann. Fifty-one years they'd been married, sharing and witnessing each other's daily lives.

And what of Will's three daughters? As you might expect, they and their husbands enjoyed Will and Ann's company. The grandchildren thrilled at their grandparents' visits. They were pleasant people to be with. As always, Will and Ann were interested in the lives of others, and that made them interesting to others.

Will continued to spend time with friends—some of them even former business associates. No one ever accused Will of "business-first" relationships. Of course, he did business, quite successfully, but he'd rather not have done business if it meant exploiting someone. It was never "just business" to Will.

Will died of heart failure just short of his 82nd birthday. In his final weeks, as he knew he didn't have long to live, his spirit grew stronger. He actually had more laughter, more joy, greater peace. Will never believed there was anything outside of himself that could make a real difference on the inside. His experience of life was marked by a vision that his life was a gift to be appreciated, and appreciate it he did. In doing so, Will became a gift to others.

The NEVER-ENDING
Search

There is always tension between the practical—having the best life experiences—and the experience of consciousness —that is, having the best experience of life. The first is all about "doing" in order to have a better life experience. The second is about "being" and enjoying the experience of your life. It's not about what you *do,* but rather what you *are* that makes the difference in your life.

And it is certainly easier to have a fine experience of life when all of life's experiences are to your liking and meet your practical desires. Yet, even for a company CEO like Will, a high proportion of day-to-day life experiences are difficult. For example, our success is always relative;

someone has always achieved more, and there's so much more to achieve. Almost immediately, we raise our expectations, and our experience of life is compromised by our dissatisfaction with what we've accomplished.

And sometimes, oftentimes, our life experiences are downright undesirable. Our loved ones get sick and die. We lose our jobs. Our kids struggle. Our own health is less than perfect. It's just the way life is. It's the Supreme Principle of the Universe.

Although most people don't realize it—and even the people who know it don't often keep it in mind—all of us are essentially seeking one thing, the same thing: the best experience of life. Most of us, without being conscious of it, seek the best experience of life by trying to have the best life experiences. We believe there are certain circumstances that will improve our experience of life. We seek to have more money, more free time, more things, better sex, more romance, better vacations, faster cars, more social status, and on and on.

And it works! For a while, at least.

You see, having better life experiences *does* improve our experience of life, if only temporarily. And that's the captivating thing about money and sex and power and all those other matters of life experience. But when the pleasure of the most recent life experience wears off, and it inevitably does, we are on the hunt again for another life experience to improve the quality of our experience of life.

Haven't we all had that experience where something or somebody we couldn't live without gives us a thrill for a while? Then after a while, as BB King might say, "the thrill is gone." The excitement fades; we have to move on to something or somebody new. The search is endless, and the demand to find a more satisfying life experience is relentless. Every life experience that satisfies temporarily only increases the demand that the next one be slightly better in order to satisfy more completely. Anything less is disappointing—or worse, demoralizing, even depressing. The rising expectations are ruthless, and the search is exhausting.

But in the world of psychology, it is widely acknowledged that the quality of our experience of life is determined not by our life experiences, but by our state of consciousness. Another way to put this is that our quality of experience of life is a function of our focus of spirit. Depending on the focus of our spirit or consciousness—i.e., what we are aware of—every moment holds the promise of being the best experience of life at that moment, apart from any circumstance. It's why Mother Theresa could live in squalor and still have a profound and even enviable experience of life.

Cosmic EQUALITY

Across cultures, regardless of gender, age, economic circumstance, education, position, power or any other variable, the only factor that really determines quality of experience of life is focus of spirit: what we are aware of, our state of consciousness. Isn't it ironic, then, that we spend so much time climbing the ladder of corporate success, chasing the almighty dollar and searching for our soul mate, when none of this will sustain us in having a satisfying experience of life? These are all part of the search for the best life experiences, but they have no long-term bearing on the best experience of life.

What we're talking about here is called the *Equalizer Principle* because everyone, regardless of circumstance, as long as he or she is not starving, has exactly the same chance for a high quality of life experience. (It does appear that those who are without sustenance are especially challenged in maintaining a decent quality of life. I would maintain that this is why it is so important for all of us, and especially those of us who value the spiritual essence of the human experience, to help feed people who are hungry and starving. By doing so, we give them the same opportunity we have for a high-quality experience of life.)

There is actually neurobiology that supports and explains this phenomenon. So as not to bore you or to risk that you will realize the rather narrow range of my knowledge on this subject, I'll keep it simple.

Basically, the excitement you feel when you experience a new and pleasurable thing in your life is the result of brain chemistry. You like the "excitement chemicals." But their effect, being subject to the Supreme Principle of the Universe—Entropy Happens—is temporary. And not only do they wear off, but they also continually require more stimulation to provide the same effect. Age also mediates the responsiveness of these neurochemical processes. So, as we age, not only does it take more stimulating activity to get the "high," but our brain is also less reactive and requires even more stimulation. It's a never-ending cycle, which is why, if neurobiological stimulation is the point of your life, the consequence is, inevitably, frustration, despair and anguish.

What I've described here is a very simple explanation of addiction. You can be addicted to anything or even anybody that becomes the pathway to the chemical stimulation and the experience you seek.

Neurobiologically speaking, then, seeking the best life experiences, chasing for chemical excitement as the point of your life, is unsustainable. Please understand, that this is not a moral or religious admonition, although it is often found in religious traditions and teachings. Regardless of what you believe, I'm presenting you with an undeniable medical fact.

But having the best experience of life, apart from depending on the best life experiences, is different. Having the best experience of life is about your state of consciousness. It's about what you "see."

Positive THINKING, *Positive* Seeing

Your state of consciousness is more than your attitude. It is true that having a positive attitude can help you to manage your experience of life. But consciousness is deeper: it is not just the way you think about things, but also the very essence of *you*. So, changing your state of consciousness involves actually seeing life from a different perspective. It is seeing life less as "doing" or having and more as "being." It is viewing yourself more as a spiritual being having a human experience than a human being having a spiritual experience. It is measuring your life less by what you accomplish and more by what life really is: a journey.

A positive attitude would seem to require self-deception. As Mihaly Csihszentmihalyi points out, if you try to apply a positive attitude with an unchanged view or perspective of life—that is, a change in your state of consciousness— you have to try to convince yourself of things that simply aren't true.[53]

For example, good health is one thing. "Good health" is when most or all health factors in your life are good. But bad health is any one of a hundred, maybe a thousand, things being wrong. To try to have a positive attitude about health without "seeing" from a different perspective is an exercise in self-deception. To be positive even when things are wrong, in a given life experience such as health, is futile. Attitude is more about putting a spin on life experiences. But it's still viewing life experiences, albeit positively viewed life experiences, as the determining factor for the best experience of life.

So, *how you see* determines *what you see*. If you see life experiences being the determining variable to your experience of life…if you see circumstantial, practical variables as the determining factors in your state of consciousness…then you will struggle to maintain a positive attitude, to convince yourself that there is a silver lining to every less-than-desirable situation. But if you can see beyond circumstance, beyond the day-to-day routine of human *doing* and have a vision of yourself as a human *being*, then *how* you're seeing your life changes *what* you see. And that makes all the difference.

Power & FLOW

The Equalizer Principle says that the quality of your life is determined by your state of consciousness. If this is true, power is a function of how many of the variables that determine your state of consciousness are inside of you, not outside of you.[54] (Remember the Principle of the Common Denominator?)

If your state of consciousness is determined by having the best life experiences—i.e., more and better of everything—then you are on an unrelenting treadmill of searching for, and acquiring, the life experiences that will only temporarily improve your experience of life. These things, whether people or material possessions or experiences, are circumstantial and, therefore, external. This leaves you dependent on those externals, often largely beyond your influence, to bring a better experience of life. Which means that, if you're depending on "stuff" to improve your experience of life, you're relatively powerless.

When you focus on internal variables, you have greater power over the quality of your life experience. This internal focus leads to the experience of what Csikszentmihalyi has named *flow*: the state of consciousness in which you are so involved in what you're being and doing that nothing else seems to matter. When you're in flow, you find the experience so enjoyable that you'll take great risk for the sake of doing it.[55]

People in flow lose track of time. They may be only slightly aware of other circumstantial issues. They're experiencing inner harmony, and they're so engrossed in what they're doing that the frustrations inherent in life are seen as challenges, but not obstacles.

Isn't this the state of consciousness you desire? And what about the people with whom you live—your spouse and kids? Wouldn't your flow experience be to their benefit too? Instead of relating to your loved ones as functionaries with duties to perform, you could encourage them, by way of example, to do what means most to them and find their own internal rewards.

The *Fourth* PRINCIPLE at Work in Your *Organization*

And what of work? What about the people who supervise us and the people we supervise? The variables that seem to inhibit this flow experience in the work environment are related to employees not having good relationships with their supervisors. The more the focus is on only the practical, the completion of tasks, rather than the inspiration that comes from mutual trust, by way of relationship, the more these employees' focus is on the external and the less they are in flow. These poor relationships result in employees who have poor interaction with management and report they often feel they don't have enough variety in their work experience or the encouragement to think for themselves.[56] This discourages problem solving and creativity. What could be worse for an organization, in this information age when ideas are a company's greatest asset, than to have legions of employees going through the motions rather than living and working with creativity and ingenuity? Of course, organizations with a "people as the strategy" philosophy would be working to remove these limiting variables, and would, therefore, be working toward establishing a "flow workplace."

So, a focus on the internal variables to determine our state of consciousness gives us great power in our lives. But what are these variables?

LIVING FROM
Within

The internal variables that affect your experience of life are often thought of in terms of character traits: honor, integrity, trustworthiness, etc. Some people think of the variables as issues of temperament, such as persistence, courage and steadfastness. Yet others may consider them to be issues of style, such as kindness, gentleness and interpersonal sensitivity.

In any case, all of these characteristics are internally determined and not circumstantially driven. Therefore, if you live from these characteristics, the quality of your life emanates from how you approach life, rather than from what happens to you in life. That's a much more powerful position from which to live.

And, while I think it is wise to consider these issues of character, temperament and style, I still believe that the variables determining your state of consciousness are really related to *seeing*: not seeing in a physical sense, or "seeing" a goal and having a vision of what you want to accomplish, but actually seeing life from a new and more profound perspective. It is "seeing" with a focus on what really matters in the experience of life. It is a way of seeing that is more about *how* we see than *what* we see.

This new way of seeing is simply a matter of *reflection* rather than reflexiveness or reaction. Most of the time, as we attend to the external variables that make up our life experiences, we react to circumstance with a sort of psychological reflex. For example, your friends buy a new car. You admire it, ride in it, drive it and, then, in a month or two, find yourself buying a new car. You don't need a new car. The one you're driving is fine. But almost reflexively, without much consideration, you fall into the trap of allowing external variables to become too prominent in your experience of life.

You actually know better. You can say, "I know the new car was unnecessary," and you can protest the idea that you made an external thing critical to your experience of life. But then, why did you buy something you clearly and admittedly didn't need? How is it that you find yourself doing so many things that, if you had stopped and reflected, you almost certainly wouldn't have done?

In a new way of seeing, the focus turns from reflex to reflection. You stand apart from yourself and reflect on the human experience. You look over the landscape of your life and consider what really matters. From ten thousand feet, you look down at the big picture. You understand that nothing and no one will be able to help you sustain a better experience of life. You recognize that what really matters comes from within.

This is maturity. It's perspective. The more reflective you are, the more powerful you can become.

We may envy people who are reflexive. They always have the quick, sharp-tongued retort. They have the newest electronic devices. They always seem hip and cool.

We may envy these people. But we *admire* people who are reflective. These are the people who seem to really have what matters. They may not be cool, but they're amazingly warm.

Please remember that the point here is that this is the Equalizer Principle: It's available to you no matter what your circumstances or station in life. You just have to be willing to see differently. And to that end, there is one variable that I, quite serendipitously, discovered to be the most significant, overriding variable affecting the quality of your life. Serendipitously for you, it's our next principle of uncommon sense.

The *Fourth* Principle
SUMMARIZED

- It's not about what you *do*, but rather what you *are*, that makes the difference in your life.

- The *Equalizer Principle* says everyone, regardless of circumstance, as long as he or she is not starving, has exactly the same chance for a high-quality experience of life.

- The quality of our experience of life is determined not by our life experiences, but by our state of consciousness; that is, by how we see the world.

- The key to having a great experience of life is the ability to see life from a different perspective. It is seeing life less as "doing" or having and more as "being." It is viewing yourself not so much as a human being having a spiritual experience, but rather as a spiritual being having a human experience.

- *How you see* determines *what you see.* If you can see beyond circumstance, beyond the day-to-day routine of human *doing* and have a vision of yourself as a human *being,* then *how* you're seeing your life changes *what* you see. And that makes all the difference.

- Please remember that the point here is that this is the Equalizer Principle: It's available to you no matter what your circumstances or station in life. You just have to be willing to see differently.

THE FIFTH
UNIVERSAL PRINCIPLE
OF UNCOMMON SENSE

THE REAL POWER

PRINCIPLE:

IT'S *only* ABOUT

RELATIONSHIPS

Steve's STORY

Several years ago, I became fascinated with the newest trend of psychological study: positive psychology. For more than a century, psychology had studied behavior and behavior change largely in the context of psychopathology —abnormal behavior—and treatment of such pathology. Theories and studies focused on trying to understand what caused people to behave in an aberrant manner and how to intervene in order to change their behavior and experience. Positive psychology—studying what made people happy—was different and, I thought, important.

About the time I was completing my personal study of the available research on happiness, my business partner Steve announced to me that he'd been feeling fatigued. He'd drawn his own blood and looked at the lab results and, based on what he saw, was going to see his internist, a colleague of ours, for a consultation.

A couple of years before, Steve had had coronary bypass surgery, so when he first started feeling fatigued this time, it only made sense that Steve thought he might have a new blockage. In fact, Steve had actually had bypass surgery twice in ninety days due to a strange autoimmune reaction that caused his grafts to close. His first thought about the fatigue was to consult with his cardiologist. He did and was told everything looked fine.

So, Steve decided to look at his blood. His blood draw confirmed that the cardiologist was right. His fatigue was not his heart, but rather something even more ominous.

Steve consulted one of the best hematologists in the Midwest, who called him on the day before his Christmas break in 2001 to tell him the test results indicated he had multiple myeloma, a form of blood or bone cancer with no known cure.

Steve was devastated. His wife, Debbie, was devastated. His family and friends were devastated. His patients were devastated. Our medical practice was devastated. And, of course, I was devastated. Steve had survived a year-long struggle with coronary disease, and the complications associated with it, and come back to continue his psychiatry practice only to be told, a little over two years later, that he had an incurable cancer.

I had never felt such helplessness in my life. I had to do something, but what? I knew Steve would get the best medical care available. He had attended medical school here in Indianapolis. Steve and I had even taught together at the medical school and had scores of physician contacts. Steve's brother, Lou, was a prominent anesthesiologist in the area, and he had several other family members in the medical community. So, the quality of Steve's medical care was almost a given. But what could *I* do?

Then, it occurred to me: I could do the research and write about the non-medical aspects of health and healing—all of those things you hear about that people claim contributed to their healing, but were outside the realm of traditional medicine. I determined that I would find the research, study it thoroughly and write what I learned for Steve. With a combination of the best medical care available and knowledge of the non-medical things that could help in his recovery, maybe, just maybe, Steve could find some remission. So, I set out on my labor of love for my friend.

I ordered dozens of books. I read dozens of articles. I chased down the most obscure studies in some of the most remote journals. I knew that Steve was a physician's physician and a scientist. He was practical and data based. No nonsense. I had to "come with the data." And I did.

I read. I read everything I could get my hands on. I got up and read at four in the morning. I read until I went to bed. I read during the day between patients and through cancelled appointments. I read in the middle of the night when I couldn't sleep. And I began to write.

Over the course of two years, I wrote Steve some 20 letters. I started with probably the best-known, non-medical intervention for incurable diseases: laughter. Dr. Norman Cousins had enlightened the world about the therapeutic value of laughter over two decades earlier. It seemed like the right place to begin.

I wrote Steve about the importance of hope and optimism, and then love and relationships. I wrote him about the findings on the importance of spirituality and faith. I wrote him of the importance of prayer.

As it became more apparent to both Steve and me how powerful this disease was, my letters, while still carrying a scientific tone, actually became more spiritual.

I don't know if any of the non-medical aspects that I wrote Steve about made any difference. He died after a two-and-a-half-year fight. Would he have died earlier? No one knows. But I know it was a profound experience for both of us to consider these issues when so much was at stake.

What follows is what these experiences taught me after he died.

The DATA on
Happiness

I mentioned that, just prior to Steve's cancer diagnosis, I began to read the expanding number of articles and books on positive psychology. The popularity of psychology, one of the fastest-growing fields of study in the twentieth century, is abundant evidence of the diligence of psychologists in studying all aspects of behavior. But most of the literature in psychology has always been devoted to the study of abnormal behavior. At the dawn of the twentieth century, few people were versed in the field.

At the turn of the last century, psychology had become the stuff of casual conversation and everyday vernacular. Consider the everyday familiarity with such terms as "ego", "depression", "anxiety" and "psychotherapy" not to mention "Prozac", "Xanax" and "Ritalin." We may not realize it—and if we realize it, we may not like it—but our culture today is steeped in psychobabble.

But curiously enough, until about twenty years ago, very few psychologists studied happiness. What are the variables that account for a person's happiness?

This question seemed important to me, and I began to study. First, I read books and articles by world-renowned social psychologist David Myers, of Hope College in Holland, Michigan. His 1993 book, *The Pursuit of Happiness*,[57] summarized the available data on the study of happiness. I read the writings of the former president of the American Psychological Association, Martin Seligman, on authentic happiness, which is, in fact, the title of one of his most popular books. I read the findings of numerous studies from dozens of authors. As the saying goes, I did my homework.

In the end, I came to realize that there are half a dozen to a dozen variables that seem to consistently account for one's happiness. These variables are universal and relevant, regardless of age, gender, race, location, educational level, culture, socioeconomic status, ability, disability or any and all other variables—except poverty. Poverty causes one to focus on trying to create a better life experience immediately, as a means of survival. Not surprisingly, poverty does impair a person's ability to have a happy experience of life.

In *The Pursuit of Happiness*, Myers claims that, as you might imagine, happy people seem to like themselves. They have better self-esteem than unhappy folks. Myers also says that these happy people believe themselves to have more influence over their own future. Whether that's actually true is not the point: It's their belief that matters. Myers says that happy people seem, by nature, to have more optimism. Happy people are more social. They are most often married. Those who experience happiness also enjoy periodic solitude. Happy people are more physically fit. And those with happiness have a belief in a faith tradition—and the more fundamental the belief, of whatever stripe, the greater the happiness.

In *Authentic Happiness*,[58] Martin Seligman claims we all have signature strengths that, when used every day in the main activities of our lives, will result in authentic happiness. He also writes of the importance of forgiveness and gratitude, as well as having a sense of "calling" in life, or using what you have in the service of something larger than you. The consequence of acting on your calling is having a meaningful life and, thus, achieving deep happiness.

Both authors and many others who write on the topic of happiness point out that seeking the satisfaction of the senses and emotions—that is, seeking pleasure—is contrary to the notion of happiness. On the other hand, they have found that seeking to enhance personal strengths and virtues, what Seligman calls gratification, is the royal road to happiness.

And it is a road that never ends. Happiness seems not to be a place at which you arrive, but rather the way to move along the road. If you look at all the factors listed above, happiness doesn't seem to be about achievement at all: It's more *how* you do things than *what* you do.

It's *Only* About RELATIONSHIPS

After Steve's death, it occurred to me that I had two lists. One was the list of six to 12 things that have been shown to be related to happiness. The other was a handful of non-medical issues that have been shown to improve health and increase the chances of survival from life-threatening disease. Two lists: factors in happiness and factors in health. This, I thought, might really be something; who doesn't want health and happiness? So, what had I learned? What *could* I learn?

I began to study the lists. I tried to identify and separate the minor factors in both lists from the more powerful predictors of happiness or health. And I looked for overlap on the lists. Were there common factors that might be held out as the most important predictors of health and happiness?

Well, certainly there were some things on one list that were not on the other. There were variables that didn't overlap; for example, having a sense of control in life seems to contribute to happiness, but I saw no evidence that suggested it could improve health. Ditto for the importance of solitude.

Then there were things that overlapped, but seemed to contribute much more to happiness than to health. Self-esteem, for example: it's heavily connected with happiness, but doesn't appear to be as critical to health and recovery.

But there was one variable that stood out both in the frequency with which it occurred on the lists, regardless of author, and the emphasis the author placed upon its importance. That factor was relationships. And this is what I mean when I say, "Life is really *only* about relationships."

It's *only* about relationships! Now, that's a bold statement. You may think I'm being simplistic. I would say that it is certainly simple, but certainly not simplistic. This realization, that the key to a satisfying experience of life is about relationships and only about relationships, was an epiphany for me, and led to the formulation of the Real Power Principle: "It's Only About Relationships." I think it can be a revelation for you, too—and lead to Real Power in your own life.

REAL *Power*

Life is only about relationships. This is a bold conclusion, to be sure. But consider that David Myers identifies this fact when he says about his research into the importance of relationships in happiness that "social support—feeling liked, affirmed and encouraged by intimate friends and family—promotes both health and happiness." His data and that of others overwhelmingly suggest that relationships have a "robust effect" in raising your level of happiness.[59]

To quote Dr. Dean Ornish, the well-known author and health expert, "I have found that perhaps the most powerful intervention—and the most meaningful for me and most of the people with whom I work, including staff and patients—is the healing power of love and intimacy, and the emotional and spiritual transformation that often results from these…. Love and intimacy are among the most powerful factors in health and illness, even though these ideas are largely ignored by the medical profession. I am not aware of any other factor in medicine —not diet, not smoking, not stress, not genetics, not drugs, not surgery—that has a greater impact on our quality of life, incidence of illness and premature death from all causes."[60]

What a powerful testament to the importance of relationships in health! And it's not from just any physician: Ornish is a world-renowned cardiologist who is considered to be one of the top 20 medical scientists of the twentieth century. He is one of the fathers of the modern healthy heart movement. He writes in advocacy of very scientific, traditional medical interventions for cardiac health; yet, when it's all said and done, he believes there's nothing, not even any medical treatment or technique, more important in health and healing than relationships!

And so, while we all readily acknowledge the importance of relationships in our lives, we may need to take a step back, reflect for a moment, and recognize that they are not just important, but are also, in fact, *the most* important factor in our health and happiness. For it is out of our loving, intimate relationships that we take better care of ourselves, that we stay active, that we remain hopeful and optimistic, that we laugh, that we have our sense of meaning. Therefore, I say boldly that life is *only* about relationships. For without good relationships, we are more likely to be unhappy and to wallow in unhappiness until we get sick and die prematurely.

And it's not just me or even just me and a bunch of scientists saying this. About two thousand years ago, there was a great sage who said there were only two things that really mattered: first, to love God with everything you have, and second, to love your neighbor as yourself. Wasn't Jesus really saying that it's only about relationships? Your relationships with a power higher than yourself, and your relationships with others in your life? Are you surprised to find so much agreement between spirituality and science?

Please note that I'm not talking about *a* relationship. As I said earlier, there is no relationship, no other person or even god, who can sustain you in a better experience of life. What I'm talking is about is loving *all*, and not necessarily anyone in particular. I'm talking about loving as a way of life, about embracing everything we've been blessed to have in our lives. That's where the Real Power resides.

The *Fifth* PRINCIPLE at Work in Your *Organization*

Recognizing the importance of relationships to the experience of life can be applied to an organization as easily as it can be applied to an individual. It's easy to see, for example, in considering a family to be a small organization. My clinical experience shows that families with a distinct, even if subtle, focus on the external—that is, on things and accomplishments—are much more fragmented than those families where relationships are primary.

When crisis comes to outer-directed families, the risk of deterioration is great. The fragmentation results in a sort of "me-against-you" approach to problem solving, rather than a healthier and more effective "we're-in-this-together" approach. And you can't change to this more effective mental framework in the middle of the crisis; it has to be the consequence of a continual historical emphasis. People don't let their guard down or stop feeling the need to look out for number one on a moment's notice. To let down your guard, you have to have a consistent sense of safety and security in your relationships.

The recent film, *The Squid and the Whale,* presents an excellent, and very accessible, example of an outer-directed family in crisis. Bernard Berkman is an author whose literary career is in decline. His wife, Joan, is a new writer whose star is on the rise. She's placed a story in *The New Yorker,* and she's sold her first novel. Joan has been an unfaithful wife for a long time; her emotionally detached relationship with her husband has led her to seek happiness elsewhere. Both people have put achievement and external validation in charge of their happiness. Even if they care about each other—and you get the sense that, in a halting and desperate way, they do—Bernard and Joan are so dependent on life experiences for their happiness that they cannot possibly cooperate to hold their disastrous marriage together, even when their children's happiness is at stake. The children, too, have learned terrible lessons from their parents, and to see them seek happiness outside themselves is even more tragic.

The Real Power Principle—or its opposite—applies to larger organizations, too. I watched one large, multi-national organization I worked with gradually shift from "people as the strategy", where their employees supported and defended their company in good times and bad, to a duplicitous position, where they said their people were their strategy, but none of their thousands of employees would have believed it. They acted in direct contradiction to their claim. Instead of honoring their people, instead of guarding their relationships first and the bottom line second, they gradually, but surely, communicated a message that the bottom line ruled and relationships were an afterthought. Long-time employees and vendors went from being loyal, committed, team players to looking out for themselves because they sensed the lack of importance the organization placed on them and their relationships with each other or the company.

Of course, the shift to a bottom-line sensibility eventually hit the bottom line. In spite of the sincere efforts on the part of the leaders of the company to protect the bottom line, they had, in fact, been negligent in best managing their most valuable assets: their relationships, their people. They blamed the market and the government and changing times, but I have not yet heard them say, "It's us. We've lost our focus on what we're really all about."

It takes years to build trust among the people of an organization, and just minutes to destroy it. And I'm talking about leaders who are brilliant people: great training, degrees and experience in the finest institutions in America. No shortage of competence here. But great leadership requires moving beyond competence. My hope is that this company's leaders come to an awareness of what's happening before the damage is irreparable. I'm not confident they will. I believe they've lost their way.

I presented the data earlier. Forty percent greater productivity and up to 50 percent greater profitability for those companies who see their people—in other words, relationships—as their strategy. Again, this is regardless of industry or market conditions. The whole idea seems unbelievable, but the data are solid, from some of the most reliable sources in the country.[61]

The Real Power Principle says that your life and happiness —and, thus, your ability to be an effective leader—are all about relationships. The Equalizer Principle says that your circumstances don't matter. So, now the question is, "what is it that makes relationships healthy?" How do you build and sustain relationships that lead to better health and happiness—not to mention better leading? What do great relationships look like?

Creating great relationships is really easy to do. But it's also easy to *not* do. And that's the problem. All of which leads us to the final uncommon-sense principle.

The *Fifth* Principle
SUMMARIZED

- The Fifth Principle of Uncommon Sense says that "life is really *only* about relationships."

- There's nothing, not even any medical treatment or technique, more important in health and healing than relationships!

- While we all readily acknowledge the importance of relationships in our lives, we may need to take a step back, reflect for a moment, and recognize that they are not just important, but are in fact *the most* important factor in our health and happiness.

- Your life and happiness—and thus your ability to be an effective leader—are all about relationships.

THE SIXTH
UNIVERSAL PRINCIPLE
OF UNCOMMON SENSE

THE PRINCIPLE OF

THE GOLDEN RULE:

LIFE IS *only* ABOUT

RELATIONSHIPS,

AND RELATIONSHIPS

ARE *all* ABOUT RESPECT

The *Obnoxious* CUSTOMER

Val is a gifted interior decorator: an artist, even considered by many who have worked with her to be a genius. Those who have the good fortune of being friends with Val are even luckier: she envelopes you in such a warm, generous and fun-loving way that you feel welcome and appreciated, no matter who you are.

Val is employed by a retailer that sells home-decorating accessories. She's obviously well placed in her position, considering her significant talent, and does her employers a great service every day she works for them. And her personable nature makes her a perfect match for retail. She draws people to her with her warm, inviting style. When clients experience her genius, they are destined to be repeat buyers.

The other day, Val told me a story that I thought profound. She said a customer, a man in his late 50s, came in wanting to buy some window coverings. The customer was edgy, ill-tempered and impatient. Val admitted that his crankiness caused her to pull back and put a damper on her typically gregarious style, but she remained kind, helpful and respectful. She was curious about why he was out of sorts, but said nothing and just remained of service to him.

This, after all, is Val's style; she's always respectful of others, regardless of how they treat her.

Val is a survivor of breast cancer. Oftentimes, something happens to people when they have to consider death from a new angle. Their perspective undergoes a profound adjustment. They are not so quick to believe that their position, their view, their perspective, is the only one or even the right one. Val is like that. She's open.

Over the course of their interaction, Val determined that what her customer really needed was vertical blinds, so she accompanied him to that area of the home decorating department. As she continued to assist him, he apparently noticed that Val became more reserved in response to his curtness. After a few minutes, the customer said, "I'm so sorry I've been short with you. I really don't know what I'm doing when it comes to home decorating. You see, my wife usually does this type of thing. She passed away a couple of weeks ago. I'm really out of my league with this stuff."

Obviously, this man was in a great deal of pain and sorrow. Without knowing his circumstances, Val continued to be respectful of him in spite of his rudeness. As a consequence, he felt safe with her, safe enough to admit his vulnerability and to place trust in her to help him not only with his home decorating needs, but also with the anguish of, for the first time, having to do what he'd always counted on his bride to do.

You see; you never know what someone else has been

through. There are an infinite number of places in an eternity of time, and you can be only in one place at any given time. Val was in one place at one time. This man was in another place and another time. Somehow, she kept that in mind and remained kind. Respect is kindness and consideration in the face of, and regardless of, circumstance. Respect is always being nonjudgmental and being nonjudgmental makes you available to others. That's pure uncommon sense—and Val has it.

What MAKES a GOOD *Relationship?*

Decades ago, my father-in-law Neil told me the upstart psychologist, that "relationships are really all about respect." Since I have a great deal of admiration and affection for Neil, I listened and made note, but moved on in my thinking. After all, Neil is a very bright guy, but he was an oil company executive, not a "shrink." I had been through years of professional training and had, even at that point, years of clinical experience. So, certainly, while I could concur that respect was important, I couldn't go so far as to believe that relationships were "all about respect." That was just too simple.

And relationships, as I'd been taught, were anything but simple; they were complicated and they were multi-faceted. I'd been taught to consider all sorts of factors when addressing relationship issues. First, of course, there is the consideration of the individuals involved. This is the psychology of relationships, and there are all-important psychological issues that must be addressed and resolved before people can have healthy relationships. Resolving these issues can take weeks, months and even years.

For example, how can a young man have a healthy relationship with a woman until he resolves his feelings concerning his over-involved, indulgent mother? How can a woman get along with other women until she's sorted out her experience with her competitive, uninvolved mother? How can a man make his own way in the world while he still has unresolved feelings of competition with his father? All of these are part of the concept of long-term, healthy relationships being the result of stable, self-confident, emotionally mature individuals relating to each other with knowledge of their psychological issues so that they can keep their neuroses from impairing their ability to relate. This idea makes perfect sense to anyone with even a basic understanding of psychology.

We give clinical labels and even popular names to the most common of these neurotic psychological phenomena. We have "Little Man Syndrome" (sometimes referred to as the "Napoleon Complex"), which says that men of small stature have a hard time in relationships with other men because they have always felt vulnerable. We believe that they compensate for their feelings of inferiority and inadequacy by being overly aggressive, trying to prove themselves equal to the task of manhood.

And we have the "Cinderella Complex" where women, no matter how competent, capable and ambitious, believe they must have a man, a Prince Charming, in their lives to take care of them. Of course, as a consequence of this neurotic pattern, these women significantly compromise their independence, submitting to the will of others and especially to the will of the man or men in their lives. Their relationships with all others, men and women, are affected by this neurosis.

Then there are cultural issues. When it comes to relationships, we must consider such socioeconomic variables as religion, education and other environmental factors. This thinking goes something like this: Compatibility is crucial to healthy relationships, and compatibility is a function of the similarity between the individuals on these key variables. We're encouraged to "stick with our own kind" because we're more likely to understand them and therefore better able to get along with them. This is sophisticated thinking, the result of deeper understanding of the psychodynamics within and between people.

Then there's the theory that having successful relationships is about having good relationship skills. Communication is the big area of focus in this viewpoint. Of course, relationships inherently involve communication, and the idea is that the better the communication skills of those involved in a relationship, the better the relationship. This seems to make perfect sense, even common sense.

Another common-sense skill that would seem to lead to better relationships is effective conflict resolution. Inevitably, in any type of relationship, there is conflict. So, it would seem that the ability to effectively address those issues causing the conflict would be absolutely critical to an effective relationship.

In romantic relationships, there's the "soul-mate" theory. This is the idea that there is another who is, by the fact of his or her inherent nature, able to relate at a deeper, more intimate level with you. Because of the depth of the connection, he or she understands you better, resulting in a better relationship.

To a lesser degree, people have a similar belief when it comes to other, non-romantic types of relationships, too. In these relationships, it's called "chemistry." Business partners may claim that the success of their business and their working relationship is due to "good chemistry."

If you've ever been in an intensely intimate, romantic relationship or experienced the synchronicity of working closely with someone who seems to be "on the same page" with you, it's logical that there are just some people who have that certain something that makes all the difference. However, the research shows that even these relationships have a half-life, meaning that the compatibility and the excitement have a timer, and that in as little as 18 months and most often within five years, even these relationships become hard work. In other words, the chemistry cannot sustain the relationship long-term. There must be more.

The TRUTH About
Relationships

Relationships have disappointment built in as a natural part of their course.[62] It is a fact that people tend to begin relationships with the highest hopes; no one gets married thinking their marriage is going to fail. This hope is called idealization, and because people are on their best behavior when relationships begin, the high hopes are reinforced and prolonged.

You tend to idealize all relationships when they begin. This is true whether the relationship is romantic or a non-romantic friendship or a work relationship. Think about it: Isn't it true that every new relationship seems to hold that promise of being "the best one yet", or at least "better than the one I just left"? Surveys of employees show that people believe their new job is their best job ever—until they've worked for their employer for six months. Then the bloom is off the rose. You've been there. We all have.

When a relationship is in an idealized state, you attribute characteristics to the other person that are actually not present. Sometimes, it's because you don't know the other person well. Other times, it's a reflection of their best behavior, which is only temporary. Or you could be experiencing an inflated awareness of an actual characteristic. In any case, disappointment is inevitable. The disappointment is simply the intrusion of reality into the idealized relationship.

You may remember the discussion of cynicism earlier in the book, and the fact that I said that cynicism is unhealthy. Lest you think that this is a cynical take on relationships, please note that confronting simple fact is not cynicism. Cynicism is expecting the worst, regardless of fact. Cynicism is pessimism.

This is reality. This is the Supreme Principle of the Universe in action: Anything with a beginning will have an end and, in between the beginning and the end, there is that inevitable process of deterioration called entropy. In the case of the human aspects of relationships, there clearly is a beginning. So, relationships fall under the jurisdiction of the Supreme Principle of the Universe.

In relationships, we call entropy *disappointment*. Nothing and no one are ideal, and if you idealize anything or anyone, you will inevitably be disappointed. Your best friend will disappoint you. Your precious children will disappoint you. Your new job will disappoint you. Even your soul mate will disappoint you.

Idealization leads to disappointment. It's not cynical. It's just fact.

The ORDEAL

Now, before you become too dismayed about your relationships sliding into disappointment, consider, as Paul Harvey says, 'the rest of the story'. Relationships are actually an ordeal.[63] They are inherently difficult. This, I imagine, is why we commonly consider that individuals in a relationship need to "resolve their issues" in order for the relationship to succeed. Or, that they are more likely to succeed if they are compatible. Or that being able to communicate effectively is critical to sustaining the relationship. Or that it's so crucial to have a soul-level connection that will overcome all obstacles and conquer all problems.

But it is in the difficulties that relationships are actually deepened. It is in realizing that relationships of all types are an ordeal, and sustaining the relationship through the ordeal, that we find the true highest point of the relationship. It may not be the point at which there is the most idealization, but it is the point of the greatest connection and the most meaning.

My friend, Steve, went through an almost unbelievable ordeal as he slowly, painfully lost his life over the course of six years. One common consequence of his cancer, multiple myeloma, is impaired kidney function. Steve's kidneys were severely affected early on in his disease;

over the last two years of his life, he had dialysis three times a week.

The three hours hooked up to the dialysis machine were long, and Steve often tried to break up the monotony by talking with friends—including me—on the phone. (Even today, I imagine Steve thanking God for cell phones.) One day, while he was on dialysis, we were talking about what he'd already been through and what he was facing: a stem cell transplant. I asked, "Don't you ever just feel like giving up?"

Steve's response was immediate and emphatic and it has stayed with me. "You know, Greg, I would. Except for one thing, one person: Debbie." He told me that through his ordeal—this untimely, miserable, gut-wrenching, exhausting ordeal—his wife, Debbie, had shown him such hope, such honor, such dignity, such compassion, such patience and such love, that he just couldn't give up. To quit would have been dishonoring her, being disrespectful of her. Because of Debbie, he had to fight. And he fought every day for another year and a half.

I know that in more than a quarter of a century together, Steve and Debbie experienced more romantic times than they did in their last six years. I know that they had certainly seen each other at their best; and, in all of the most conventional ways, their last six years together could not have been considered their best. And I know that they still had personal characteristics that clashed, faults that never went away, and issues that were never resolved. Yet, in spite of all of these issues that affect every couple and the grinding agony of Steve's illness and Debbie's coping with his illness, their experience of the relationship in their last six years together was the best it had ever been. Through their ordeal, they grew past idealization, past compatibility, past even trying to resolve their human faults. In the end, they could clearly see that their relationship was based on the Principle of the Golden Rule: do unto others as you would have them do unto you. Treat other people the way you want to be treated.

Steve and Debbie were able to realize what was really worth living and dying for: their relationship. And the single most important aspect of all relationships is not compatibility or ardor or chemistry. It's respect.

Finally, Some DATA

Anecdotes can inspire you, make you laugh, make you cry, point you in a different direction. But are there data that back up the Principle of the Golden Rule? Are successful relationships really all about respect?

Yes. We now understand, thanks to researcher Dr. John Gottman, what the critical ingredient is that successfully propels people through the ordeal of relationship. Gottman completed a 25-year, longitudinal study of the most significant and foundational relationship known to humans: marriage[64] In spite of the fact that psychologists, social workers, clergy and many others, were spending thousands of dollars to be trained in marital therapy, no one had ever done a thorough, longitudinal study to discover the real difference between relationships that succeed and those that fail. Theories abounded, but data were lacking.

Gottman and his assistants found that there was a single characteristic that best explained the success of relationships and, in a word, that characteristic was *respect*. Gottman's study was about marital relationships, but I believe his findings are largely applicable to all relationships: parent-child relationships, friendships, coworker relationships, supervisee-supervisor relationships, business partnerships and any other relationships you'd care to consider. The universal ingredient making any and all relationships functional over the long haul is respect.

These days, I have greater admiration than ever for my oil company executive father-in-law, Neil. He told me years earlier that "relationships were really all about respect." He knew this without the data. But how? How had he seen through all of those other variables, all of the complexities of relationships, to see that respect was the key?

Well, for one thing, Neil has always been one of those people with a seemingly innate understanding of uncommon sense, a leader who inspired those in his charge. Real leadership and uncommon sense go hand in hand.

R-E-S-P-E-C-T

Gottman's work offers some detail about what is meant by "respect" in a relationship. He writes extensively about the many variables he believes are associated with respect and how these variables work to enhance marital relationships.

But it seems to me that the single characteristic common to all variables of respect, which is mentioned by Gottman as central to healthy relationships, is the willingness to be influenced by another.[65] There is nothing more inspiring to another person than the belief that he or she has enough of your respect to influence you. In turn, your respect inspires *them* to be willing to be influenced by *you*. In being willing to be influenced by others, we also see the application of the first principle of uncommon sense: The Principle of the Harvest. Simply put, you get what you give; by being willing to be influenced, you become more influential. And, of course, this ability to influence and inspire others—the ability to persuade them to willingly participate in the accomplishment of something greater than anyone thought possible—is the cornerstone of transformational leadership.

In being willing to be influenced by another, you create an openness that is critical to fostering respect. This idea of "openness" has been a part of the corporate leadership trend for years now, as even mega-corporations have tried to institute "open-door" policies. "Transparency" in communication has been a corporate buzzword for a number of years. Another aspect of openness is the idea of communicating to employees that they are respected and valued.

Openness is about accessibility and a willingness to hear what someone has to say, but it's also more. When you're open, you're not defensive. You have no need to blame or defend. You can address issues without looking for fault.

Respect means relating to others, not in terms of their behavior or your own social values or their social standing, but recognizing that beyond *doing,* beyond what we see of another, there is a human *being.* In *being,* we are all equal. In *being,* we can always honor another, even when the more functional aspects of the relationship are problematic. In *being,* we all have an influence to bring to everyone we meet. There may be coincidental relationships, but there are no accidental relationships. In being, we appreciate the worth of everyone in our lives.

Please recognize that I'm not suggesting that we agree with, accept or approve of the positions that others have or promote. In fact, it's highly unlikely you'll agree on most topics with most of the people you meet. But that's the whole point of respect. Respect is beyond judgment—so agreement, acceptance or approval is not really relevant. When you offer respect—that is, you

allow yourself to be influenced by others—you honor
their essential worth, even in disagreement or disapproval
with their position or disapproval of their actions.
You simply appreciate their presence in your life.

It is this respect that really sustains you through the
ordeal of relationship and life. Conversely, the lack of
respect explains the emptiness and loneliness that so
often plague the people who seem always to find reasons
why friendships, partnerships and relationships of all
sorts must end.

Being respectful is also about being kind in how
you deal with others. Unkindness is always born out of
insecurity. Unkind people are those who, for some reason,
believe that there is something wrong with them.
For example, lots of unkindness occurs when people
feel resentful or threatened or otherwise insecure.
Some people are unkind because they apparently think
they're better than others—and to harbor an opinion
of yourself that's based on the relative worth of others is,
by definition, a show of your own insecurity.

So, what do we know about respect? It's about being
open to influence from others. It's about honoring
people and human *beings* without judging what they're
thinking or doing. It's about simple kindness. It is, as the
Principle of the Golden Rule says, treating others exactly
as you would wish to be treated.

The *Sixth* PRINCIPLE
at Work in Your
Organization

In his studies on successful relationships, Gottman says
that disrespect is characterized by criticism, contempt,
defensiveness and harsh startups.[66] Since disrespect is
what we want to avoid, let's briefly examine each of these
phenomena. And since organizational leadership is
primarily what we're concerned with here, let's examine
them in the context of the workplace.

First, there is no room for criticism when you have
nonjudgmental, positive regard for others. You certainly
don't have to accept what they believe or say. You don't
have to agree with everyone about everything. But you
do have to respect their basic honor. Remember that,
especially with the people you lead, you should never
confuse the message with the messenger. There are
certainly times when you must offer suggestions for
improvement and even reject employees' work outright.
But remember that the person behind the work is not
the work.

Gottman says that contempt is probably the worst sort
of disrespect because it's a kind of disgust of and for
another person. When you appreciate people not for

what they do or who they are, but for the fact that they are in your life for a reason—that is, to have an influence on you in some way—you appreciate their being. It's hard to be contemptuous of people when you consider their presence purposeful.

Defensiveness, according to Gottman, is the way we blame others. Stop and consider that, when you defend yourself, you're essentially making the situation someone else's problem—most likely, the person to whom you're defending yourself. To be defensive is in contradiction with the Principle of the Common Denominator (work harder on yourself than anything else): If you are not the solution, then you don't have a problem. When you're open, you're willing to address problems without getting caught up in the blaming, which allows you to communicate a readiness to be influenced and a respect for the dignity of others. This openness is invaluable when dealing with potentially thorny issues in the workplace.

Finally, Gottman claims that the negativity of what he calls "harsh startups" in interactions is so destructive that he can predict the outcome of a fifteen-minute conversation by observing the first three minutes—with 96-percent accuracy. In other words, an unkind beginning to an interaction is almost impossible to overcome. Think, for example, of the last time a meeting you attended began with an accusation or conflict. Even if cooler heads prevailed by the time the meeting ended, no one really left the meeting feeling good about the outcome.

This is why kindness is so critical in having positive interactions with others. It's equally difficult to overcome kindness when The Principle of the Golden Rule is your approach to relationships.

All THINGS *New*

In our rapidly shrinking world, where people of wide-ranging backgrounds and cultures live and work together, it's becoming increasingly important that leaders—and remember, all of us are leading a life and influencing others—be able to appreciate personal differences and allow themselves to be influenced by those they're leading. Why? Because as the world shrinks and our information base expands, the organizations you're part of, from families to multi-national corporations, will succeed or fail, based more on the quality of the relationships they foster than any other factor.

It seems ironic, then, to consider that this sixth principle of uncommon sense is actually one of the oldest and most basic principles of all five major faith traditions in the world, and can also be found in many of the world's lesser-known belief systems. All things new are actually all things old, and having respect for others is no exception. For what we've really been talking about here, with regard to respect and the willingness to be influenced by others, is the Golden Rule.

Stated in a simple form that most of us have heard a hundred times before, the Golden Rule is, "Do unto others as you would have them do unto you." Treat others—*all* others—with the kind of respect you'd like to receive. You like to think what you say and do can influence others; give others the same opportunity to influence you. You believe your opinions about politics and religion and baseball are right. Allow others the nobility of their own opinions.

Let me put it another way by going back to a story I've mentioned throughout this book: the story of my friend Steve. How would you treat your life partner if he or she were dying of cancer? Wouldn't you be supportive, encouraging, steadfast, loyal and positive? Wouldn't you try to find positive energy in your lives? Wouldn't you keep hope alive?

The real beauty—the real genius—of my friend Steve is that *he* was the person battling cancer. And *he* extended those same positive qualities, those same measures of respect, to his wife, Debbie. Although he was not a religious man, and he would probably not have thought to imagine that what he was doing was exemplifying the Golden Rule, Steve nonetheless understood the *Principle* of the Golden Rule. He allowed himself to be influenced by Debbie, to the point that he would not give up the fight, even when giving up seemed like a real option.

We're all mortal. We're all subject to entropy. And our state of consciousness is really what determines the quality of our experience of life. And the more you understand that the variables that determine your state of consciousness are inside of you, the more powerful you are. And when you consider the two most often cited critical elements for a good life—health and happiness— the one major variable they have in common is relationships. And now we see that good relationships are sustained by a single variable: respect.

In a way, everything comes down to the Principle of the Golden Rule. If you treat people the way you want to be treated, your relationships *will* be the most important things in your life. You *will* understand that everyone has an equal chance at happiness. You *will* see the effects of entropy and pay more attention to your spirit. You *will* stop pushing blame onto others and work harder on yourself than anything else. And, of course, you *will* see that the way you treat people today affects the way you're treated tomorrow. In a way, the Sixth Principle of Uncommon Sense is both the first and the last principle. It's the one that not only works with all the others, but also incorporates them all. Which means that if you truly understand and embrace this one, the others will fall into place.

The *Sixth* Principle
SUMMARIZED

- We commonly know the Sixth Principle of Uncommon Sense as "the Golden Rule": "Do unto others as you would have others do unto you." My interpretation of this is that "life is *only* about relationships, and relationships are *all* about respect."

- Relationships are actually an ordeal. They are inherently difficult.

- It is in realizing that relationships of all types are ordeals and in sustaining the relationship through the ordeal that we find the true highest point of the relationship. It may not be the point at which there is the most idealization, but it is the point of the greatest connection and the most meaning.

- A single characteristic that best explains the success of relationships is *respect*.

- There is nothing more inspiring to another person than the belief that he or she has enough of your respect to influence you.

- Simply put, you get what you give; by being willing to be influenced, you become more influential.

- Respect is beyond judgment, so agreement, acceptance or approval is really not relevant. When you offer respect—that is, you allow yourself to be influenced by others—you honor their essential worth, even in disagreement or disapproval with their position or disapproval of their actions. You simply appreciate their presence in your life.

- This ability to influence and inspire others—the ability to persuade them to willingly participate in the accomplishment of something greater than anyone thought possible—is the cornerstone of transformational leadership.

- "Do unto others as you would have them do unto you." Treat others—*all* others—with the kind of respect you'd like to receive. You like to think what you say and do can influence others; give others the same opportunity to influence you. If you truly understand and embrace this principle, the other five will fall into place.

EPILOGUE:
WHAT NOW?

Be the *Leader* YOU *Wish* to BECOME

So, where are we now? What are we supposed to have learned on this journey? Let's regroup once again before we close.

The First Principle of Uncommon Sense, the Principle of the Harvest, says you reap what you sow. You get what you give—the same as you give, more than you give, later than you give.

The Second Principle of Uncommon Sense, the Principle of the Common Denominator, says you need to work on yourself harder than you work on anything else. *You* are the only constant in every area of your life that needs work: for better and worse, it really *is* all about you.

The Third Principle of Uncommon Sense, the Supreme Principle of the Universe, says everything that has a beginning has an end and is subject to entropy. In accepting entropy, you can also engage in negentropy and simplification to reduce its effects in your life. But you'll never defeat entropy; it is, after all *the* Supreme Principle of the Universe. What you *can* do is pay more attention to the only thing in your life that is not, for all we know, subject to entropy: your consciousness, or spirit.

The Fourth Principle of Uncommon Sense, the Equalizer Principle, says how you see is what you see. No matter what your age, sex, race, religion, country of origin, or financial status—unless it's abject poverty—you have an equal chance for happiness with everyone else in the world. It's a matter of paying attention to your experience of life, not your temporary, ever-changing life experiences.

The Fifth Principle of Uncommon Sense, the Real Power Principle, says life is all about relationships and *only* about relationships. People who have good relationships in their lives are happier and healthier—period. Your relationships are where your real power lies.

Finally, the Sixth Principle of Uncommon Sense, the Principle of the Golden Rule, says that good relationships are all about respect. If you treat people the way you wish to be treated yourself—if you allow yourself to be open and influenced by others—you'll influence others, as well. Even more important, you'll achieve the sort of happiness that's virtually impossible without good relationships.

Did I say "virtually" impossible? Strike the "virtually."

Over the course of this book, I've told some stories. I've quoted studies. I've shared thoughts from the authors of other leadership books. I've tried to load this book with ammunition to back up every claim I'm firing at you.

But remember: I've also experienced these principles in real life. I've worked with world-class leaders and homeless people, teenagers and seniors, I've worked with people so full of life that they seemed to float above the floor, and people halfway through death's door. Every one of these people was looking to be led out of a situation that brought them to my psychotherapy practice. That's why leadership has always seemed important to me.

And so, I return to where I began. There are *thousands* of books on leadership on the market today; and yet, everyone is still looking for the *next* leadership book. And even in the face of *all this material,* we continue to have a shortage of real leading. We have so many with titles and positions, so many people with leadership competence, and most people *still* feel dissatisfied with the leaders they have to deal with on their jobs?

And then, to paraphrase John Lennon, life happens while you're making plans. I mean, in the midst of all of your life planning and your day-to-day living and your pursuing matters of competence in trying to be a good leader at work and at home and in other areas of your life, changes occur and losses mount and you realize that *you are leading a life—and that the way you lead your life is the way you will lead—period.*

If we can trust the dictionary definition of *lead*—to "go through" and to "direct the actions of others by example"—we're all leaders. You can be a good leader or a bad leader, an enlightened leader or a dull, backward leader. You can lead people astray or you can lead them to the mountaintop. And it all rests on the way you lead your life. But, make no mistake: *you* are a leader. Your life *is* an example to someone. We're all leaders in this sense. But few of us see ourselves as such.

And few of us make the connection between leading a life and leading a family or a company or a department or a team. But the connection is there, regardless of whether we recognize it or not. You can't be a dictatorial father and an even-handed, democratic manager. You can't foster great relationships with your kids and run your department based on fear and loathing. I've never seen it happen—not once in all the years and all the hours I've spent dealing with these issues.

It really comes down to this: after 25 years and more than 60,000 hours of listening to patients and trying to help them understand and deal with the challenges in their lives, what I know for sure is that leadership has far more to do with *what you are* than *what you do*. The focus of so much leadership training is about how to "do" leadership. But it's about more than "doing." I've also learned that leadership is more about *what you are* than *who you are*—that is, whom you know or what position you hold. You can do all the training, networking and corporate ladder climbing you want, but none of it will make you a better, more effective leader.

We can become pretty obsessed with "doing" in this culture; I would guess that a large percentage of us start and end our days with to-do lists. And we are certainly quick to think of ourselves in terms of whom we know or what position we hold. But the studies on leadership, in every type of organization from the family to the boardroom of the largest corporations on Earth, don't back up the idea that great leaders "do" anything in common, in spite of all the books and training programs and motivational speakers who would have us believe otherwise.

So, what is leadership if not about skill, position, networking or power? If leadership is about *what you are*…well, what does that mean?

To be sure, *what* you are is something deeper and more essential—and a bit more difficult to define. It's a way of being. And so, in a profound sense, leadership is about being a leader, leading a life, before doing anything.

And what in the world does this mean? It means that leading is not only about your skills and abilities, but also, and more importantly, about the influential power of trust in relationships. It's recognizing that we manage only ourselves. To be trusted by others, we must be worthy of trust—trustworthy. We are trustworthy only when we demonstrate that we are living by a reality that is *uncommon sense*. This is a reality that inspires a view of life that is bigger than "what's in it for me." It's a reality that influences others, whether family, friends or co-workers, to participate with us in accomplishing whatever we set out to do.

Leading by *what you are* is about realizing that you already have everything you need to be everything you need to be. There is a power that lies at the center of your being, a way of "seeing" that makes everything you are and everything you do more profound because it encourages you to be what you really are.

And leading by being *what you are* requires reflection on the reality beyond the reality that is before your eyes. You must recognize that what you see, what you sense, is only a very small portion of what there is out there—and not the most important part, either. There is an *uncommon sense* that actually makes *more* sense. If you see this reality, you live and lead a different, more meaningful life.

In leading a life of uncommon sense, you recognize that you exist in an orderly universe. The extent to which you recognize that the actions of today will, in large degree, determine your life experiences and even your experience of life tomorrow, is the extent to which you are a powerful, transformational leader.

In leading a life of uncommon sense, you accept that you are the solution to all of your problems. This is the most empowering reality, and all too often forgotten. If you are not the solution to your problem, then you don't have a problem.

In leading a life of uncommon sense, you stay active, keep life simple and remember if it's created, it will end—and, in between beginning and ending, entropy will rule. To live by spirit—consciousness, as the scientists prefer to call it, the only aspect of ourselves that is apparently not created and apparently has no end—is to grow stronger with age. In spite of the effect of aging on our senses, our mobility and even our cognition, our spirit can provide us with a timeless vitality that knows no earthly bounds.

In leading a life of uncommon sense, you are always, in every minute, only a shift in focus of consciousness away from the best experience of life that anyone, no matter their station or situation, could ever hope to have. You hold within you a power for life that is truly astounding. And, almost no matter what your life experience, there is always hope for you and for others.

In leading a life of uncommon sense, you know that life is *only* about relationships. A friend of mine named Jay lost his wife to cancer a few years ago. He told me that Beth and he mutually experienced what he referred to as the "tunnel of death." He explained how, as this bright, highly educated, accomplished, vivacious woman now ravaged by the cancer drew closer to her death, the experience of life that mattered became increasingly clear, and their lives became *only* about relationships. You can always use death as your counselor when considering your priorities. It's not morbid, but realistic and practical. To quote an old cliché, no one announces on his deathbed that he wishes he'd spent more time at the office. As Tim McGraw sings about what Tug McGraw, his baseball-star father, told him, "I wish you could live like you knew you were dying."

And since life is *only* about relationships, then it's important, in leading a life of uncommon sense, to know that relationships are *all* about respect. To be open and non-defensive with others requires that we put no faith in our judgment. We simply don't know the details of another's experience or ultimate outcome, for good or ill—most likely, for good *and* ill—of any action. So, we strive to be open to influence by others, not necessarily to agree or accept, but to be respectful of the fact that we are all travelers on this journey, and we're having this experience together.

It might occur to you that there are people in positions of authority who are poor examples, destructive leaders, even people we fundamentally find repugnant. What do we do then? Well, the uncommon-sense principles still apply. If you fail to stand for what is just and fair, then you can expect to have little support when you are on the receiving end of injustice. It is the Principle of the Harvest. So, you must stand for that which you believe is right: You must always stand for justice, knowing that you are planting the seeds of a more agreeable harvest for yourself.

But in making that stand, always first consider what *you* can do to improve the injustice. This is the Law of the Common Denominator. Don't be captivated by this moment of circumstance, but rise above: take the high road. And always remember that the real strength in standing against an unjust authority is in relationship. And relationships are all about respect—not agreement, but always respect. The distressing thing about the current culture in our country is not that people disagree, but that they so often disagree so disrespectfully. Tyranny thrives in an atmosphere of disrespect.

This uncommon-sense view of life makes all the difference. Leading a life becomes less about doing, less about transactions, and more about being, more about the transformation. You are a spiritual being having a human experience. This is living from that consistent part of you that you've known all your life, when you were five years old and 15 years old, when you were 25 and 50, when you were 60 and 83 and even 100 years old. No matter what your age or the circumstances of your life, there is this part of you that you've always known was you. And it doesn't change; it's always the same, regardless of events or situations in your life. This is your being, your consciousness; and this part of you instinctively understands the uncommon-sense principles. But because most of us don't live from this foundation of *what we are*, these sensible principles are an uncommon way of life.

Back near the start of this book, I said you don't have to *do* anything. I think you can see what I meant: leadership is not about what you do. Even so, what are you supposed to do now?

Lead as you live, live as you lead. Go ahead and develop all those competencies you need to get the work done—but understand that true transformational leadership is about *what you are*. To be an inspiring leader, you have to lead an inspired life. *Be* the leader you want to become. That's all you have to do. If they make sense to you—and I hope they do—incorporate the Six Principles of Uncommon Sense into your view of the world. Then just be.

NOTES

1 Barbara Mackoff, Editorial Review, Amazon.com, 2005

2 Robert E. Quinn, Change the World: How Ordinary People Can Accomplish Extraordinary Results, 2005

3 Ibid.

4 Alice Calaprice, The New Quotable Einstein (Princeton University Press and Hebrew University of Jerusalem), 2005.

5 Redford Williams and Virginia Williams, Anger Kills (HarperCollins Publishers), 1998.

6 Michael Hitt, J. Stewart Black and Lyman W. Porter, Management (Pearson Prentice Hall), 2005.

7 Ibid.

8 Robert H. Rosen, Leading People (Penguin Group), 1996.

9 Michael Hitt, J. Stewart Black and Lyman W. Porter, Management (Pearson Prentice Hall), 2005.

10 Michael Hitt and R. D. Ireland, The Essence of Strategic Leadership: Managing Human and Social Capital, Journal of Leadership and Organizational Studies 9, 2002.

11 Corporate Executive Board, (executiveboard.com), 2004.

12 Bill Kowalski, The Engagement Gap (workindex.com), 2002.

13 Truenorth Leadership, (truenorthleadership.com), 2004.

14 Marcus Buckingham, First, Break All the Rules (Simon & Schuster), 1999.

15 Marcus Buckingham and Donald Clifton, Now, Discover Your Strengths (Simon & Schuster), 2001.

16 Redford Williams and Virginia Williams, Anger Kills (HarperCollins Publishers), 1998.

17 Robert H. Rosen, Leading People (Penguin Group), 1996.

18 Ibid.

19 Douglas McGregor, The Human Side of Enterprise (McGraw-Hill), 1985.

20 Jeffrey Pfeffer, The Human Equation (Harvard Business School Press), 1998.

21 Jeffrey Pfeffer and Robert I. Sutton, The Knowing-Doing Gap (Harvard Business School Press), 2000.

22 Abraham Maslow, Motivation and Personality (Harper), 1954.

23 Jim Collins, Good to Great (HarperCollins Publishers), 2001.

24 Jeffrey Pfeffer, The Human Equation (Harvard Business School Press), 1998.

25 Robert H. Rosen, Leading People (Penguin Group), 1996.

26 Frederick F. Reichheld, Loyalty Effect (Harvard Business School Press), 1996.

27 Jeffrey Pfeffer, The Human Equation (Harvard Business School Press), 1998.

28 Frederick F. Reichheld, Loyalty Rules (Harvard Business School Press), 2001.

29 Jeffrey Pfeffer, The Human Equation (Harvard Business School Press), 1998.

30 Ibid.

31 Tom Peters, The Circle of Innovation (Alfred A. Knopf), 1997.

32 Robert H. Rosen, Leading People (Penguin Group), 1996.

33 Huston Smith, The Soul of Christianity (HarperCollins Publishers), 2005.

34 James O. Prochaska, John C. Norcross and Carlo C. DoClemente, Changing for Good (Simon & Schuster), 1994.

35 Ibid.

36 Ibid.

37 Ibid.

38 Ibid.

39 Ibid.

40 Stephen R. Covey, The Seven Habits of Highly Effective People (Simon & Schuster), 1989.

41 Charles F. Stanley, Financial Wisdom (In Touch Ministries), 1998.

42 Jeffrey Pfeffer, The Human Equation (Harvard Business School Press), 1998.

43 Ibid.

44 Mihaly Csikszentmihalyi, Flow (Harper Perennial), 1990.

45 Jim Rohn, Take Charge of Your Life (Nightingale-Conant), 1998.

46 Mihaly Csikszentmihalyi, The Evolving Self (Harper Perennial), 1993.

47 Brian Greene, The Fabric of the Cosmos (Vintage), 2005.

48 David Blumenthal, Personal Conversations, 2003.

49 Mihaly Csikszentmihalyi, The Evolving Self (Harper Perennial), 1993.

50 Harry Beckwith, What Clients Love (Warner Business Books), 2003.

51 Joshua Halberstam, Work (Perigee), 2000.

52 David Blumenthal, Personal Conversations, 2005.

53 Mihaly Csikszentmihalyi, The Evolving Self (Harper Perennial), 1993.

54 Ibid.

55 Mihaly Csikszentmihalyi, Flow (Harper Perennial), 1990.

56 Mihaly Csikszentmihalyi, Good Business (Penguin Books), 2003.

57 David Myers, The Pursuit of Happiness (Avon Books), 1993.

58 Martin E. P. Seligman, Authentic Happiness (Simon & Schuster) 2002.

59 David Myers, The Pursuit of Happiness (Avon Books), 1993.

60 Dean Ornish, Love and Survival (HarperCollins Publishers), 1997.

61 Jeffrey Pfeffer, The Human Equation (Harvard Business School Press), 1998.

62 M. Scott Peck, The Road Less Traveled (Simon & Schuster), 1978.

63 Joseph Campbell, The Power of Myth (Apostrophe S Productions), 1990.

64 John Gottman and Nan Silver, The Seven Principles for Making Marriage Work (Weidenfeld & Nicolson), 1999.

65 Ibid.

66 Ibid.